MACHINERY AND MECHANICAL DEVICES

A Treasury of Nineteenth-Century Cuts

Selected and Arranged by
WILLIAM ROWE

DOVER PUBLICATIONS, INC.
NEW YORK

PUBLISHER'S NOTE

Rapid advances in technology in the nineteenth century led to the invention of an amazing variety of hitherto undreamt-of machines to perform a vast assortment of tasks. The Victorians (including nineteenth-century Americans) were fascinated by this new age of machines that they had created, and their books and periodicals, such as *Scientific American*, often featured detailed illustrations of the new machinery in all its staggering complexity. The result was a legacy of fine wood engravings of machines of all kinds (the wood engraving being, before the perfection of the halftone, the principal means of mass-reproducing illustrations in the nineteenth century).

Now, a century later, these engravings have stimulated the imagination of designer William Rowe, who has selected a multitude of images, many from now-rare sources, and created from them sixty fascinating and witty collages with amusing captions. Designers, illustrators, craftspeople, or anyone searching for illustrations of machines may use these images for decoration, advertising, or any other purpose. Each amusing surrealistic composition may of course also be enjoyed for itself.

Machinery and Mechanical Devices: A Treasury of Nineteenth-Century Cuts is a new work, first published by Dover Publications, Inc., in 1987.

DOVER *Pictorial Archive* SERIES

This book belongs to the Dover Pictorial Archive Series. You may use the designs and illustrations for graphics and crafts applications, free and without special permission, provided that you include no more than four in the same publication or project. (For permission for additional use, please write to Dover Publications, Inc., 31 East 2nd Street, Mineola, N.Y. 11501.)

However, republication or reproduction of any illustration by any other graphic service whether it be in a book or in any other design resource is strictly prohibited.

Manufactured in the United States of America
Dover Publications, Inc., 31 East 2nd Street, Mineola, N.Y. 11501

Library of Congress Cataloging-in-Publication Data

Rowe, William, 1946–
  Machinery and mechanical devices.

  (Dover pictorial archive series)
  1. Machinery—History—Pictorial works. 2. Engraving—
19th century. I. Title. II. Series.
TJ19.R67 1987   621.8'09'034   87-8893
ISBN 0-486-25445-3 (pbk.)

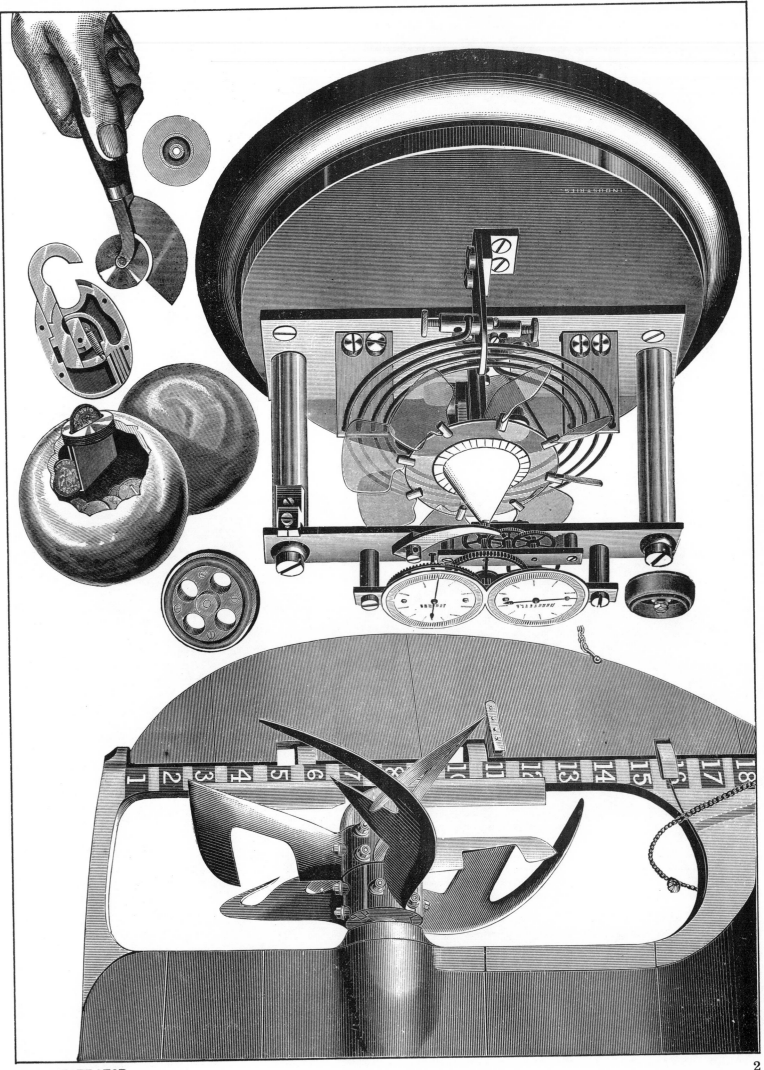

GAS REGULATOR.

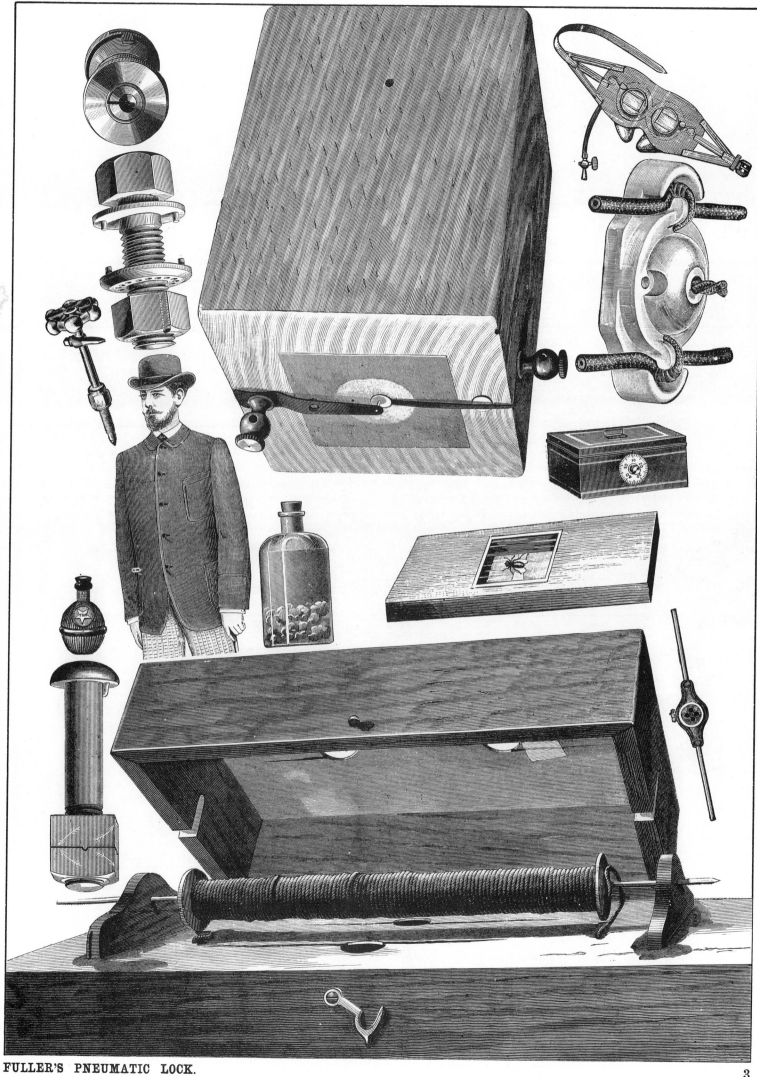

FULLER'S PNEUMATIC LOCK.

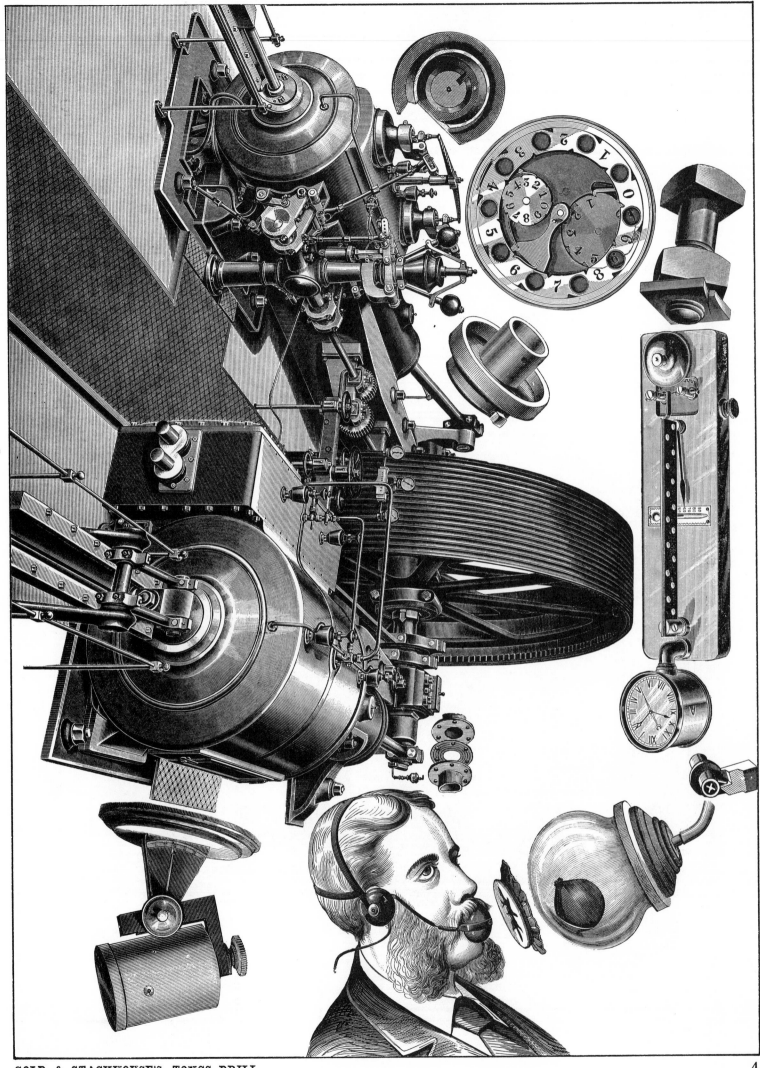

GOLD & STACKHOUSE'S TONGS DRILL.

WYSS AND STUDER'S WATER-PRESSURE ENGINE

LEUCHTWEISS' IMPROVED ROTARY PUMP.

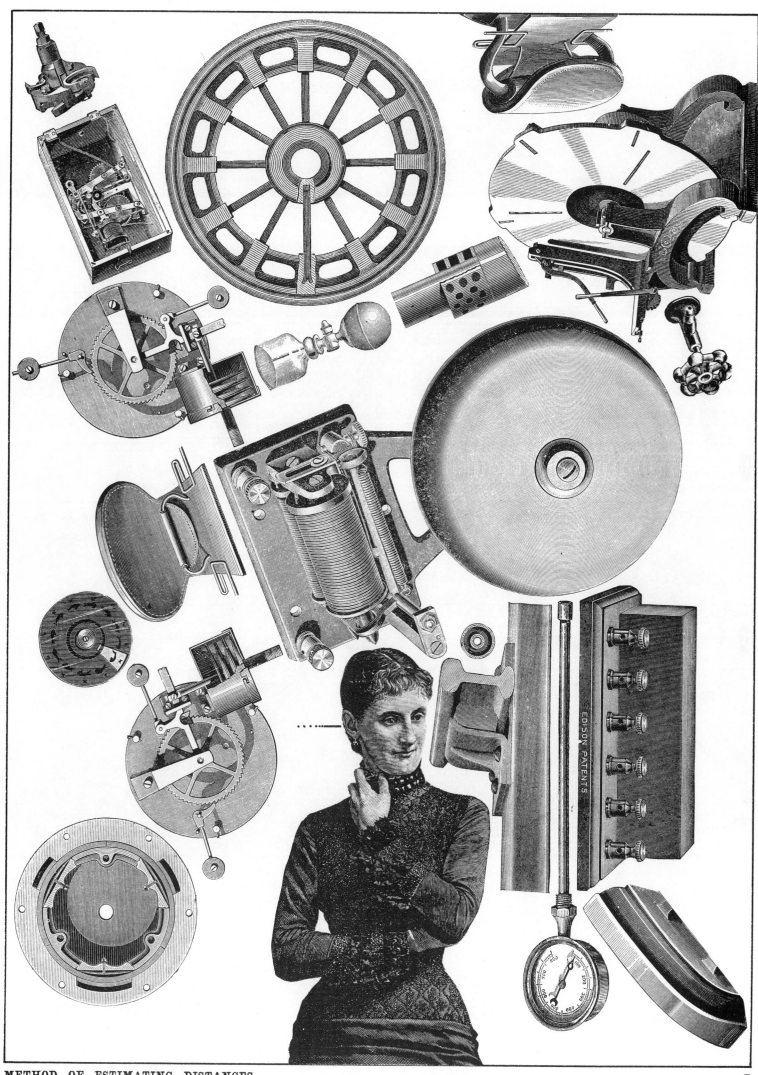

DOUBLE SHEARING, PUNCHING AND STRAIGHTENING MACHINE.

THE BURDGE PATENT IMPROVED TOOL REST.

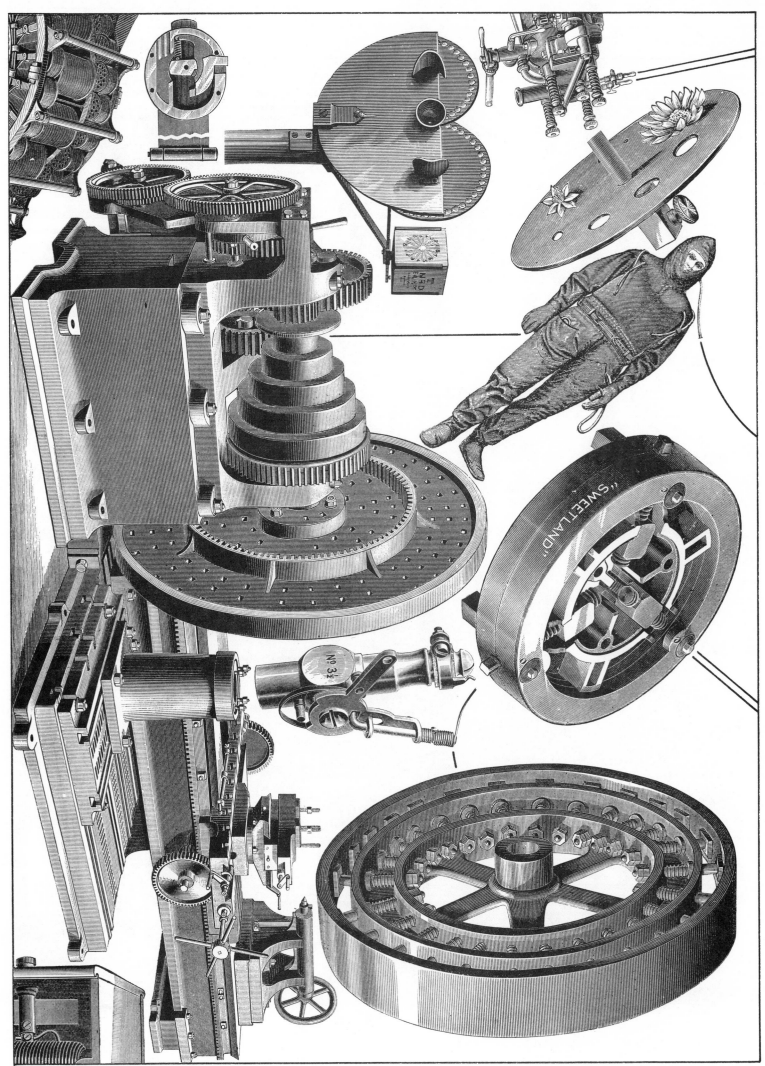

WARDWELL'S ADJUSTABLE BENCH JACK.

WEBB'S WHEEL FINISHING MACHINE.

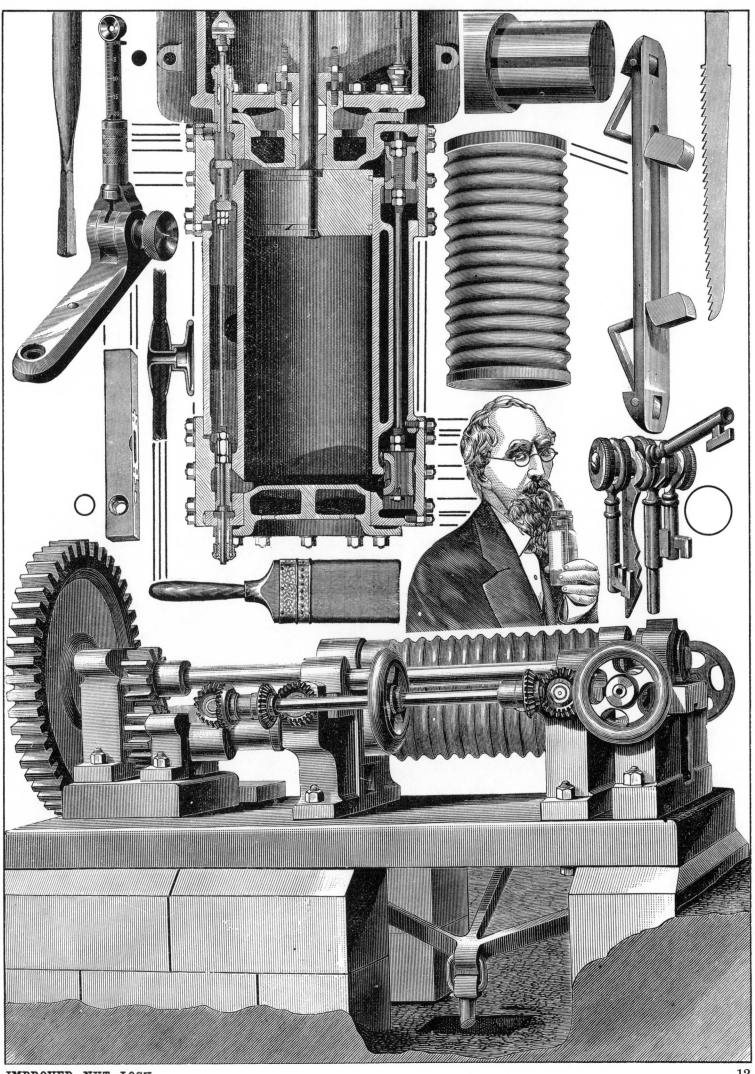

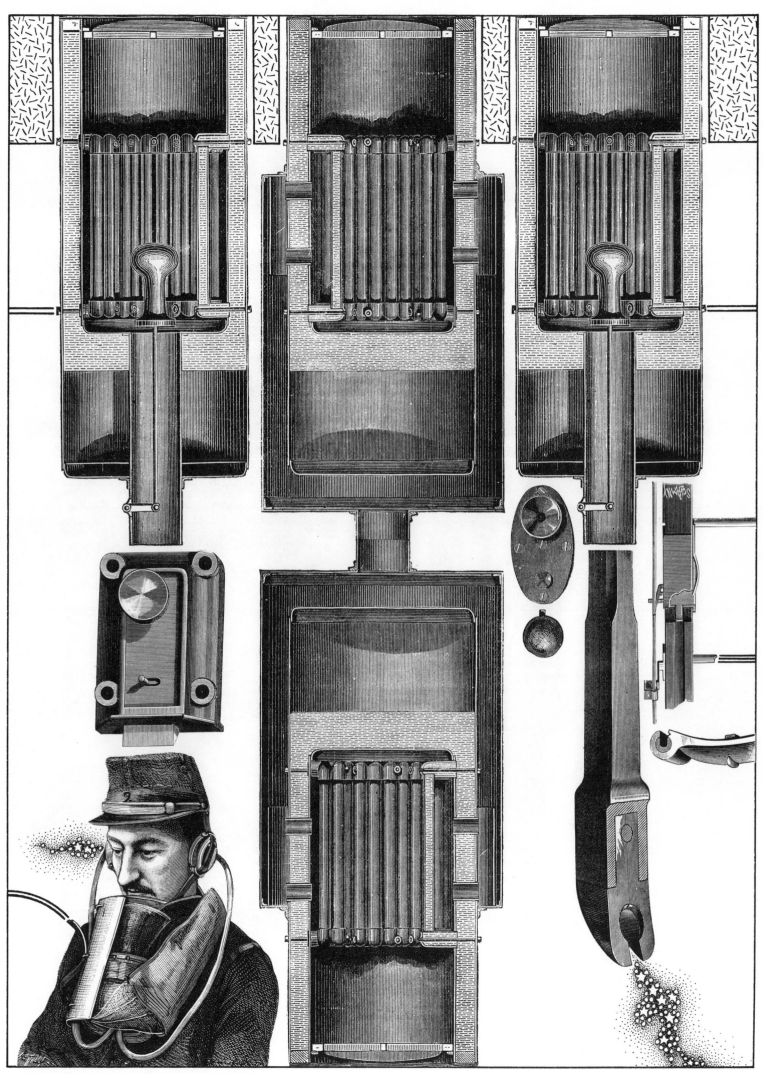

APPARATUS FOR HYDRATING LIME.

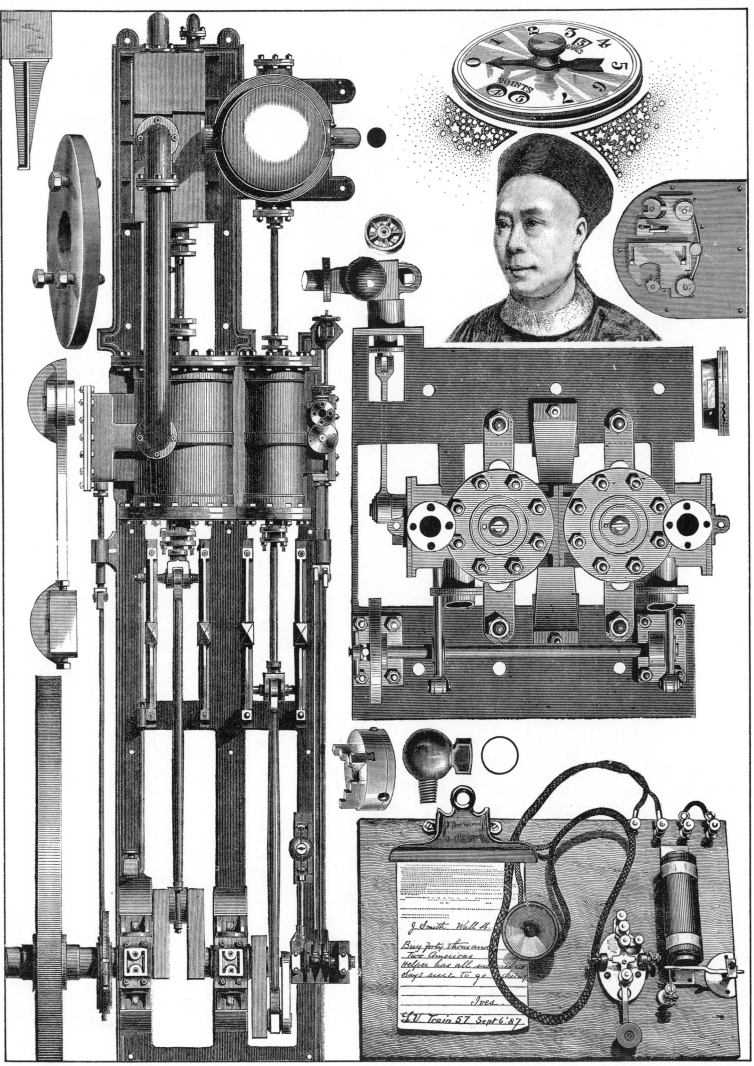

THE LIGHTNING SCREW PLATE.   14

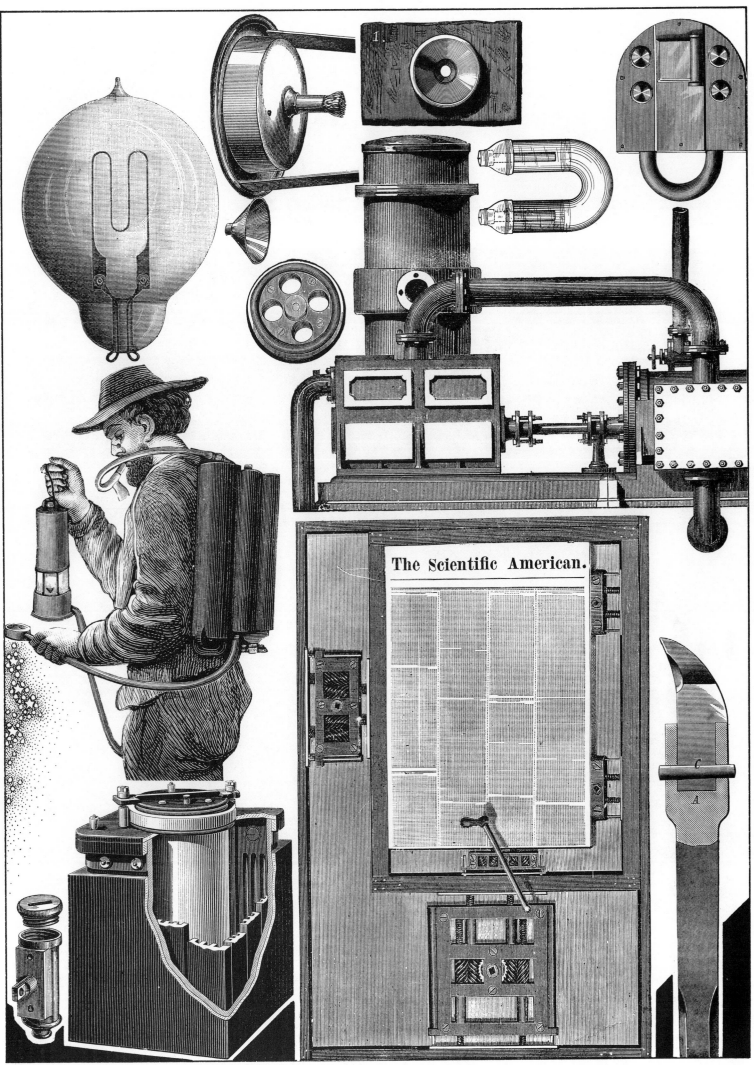

The Scientific American.

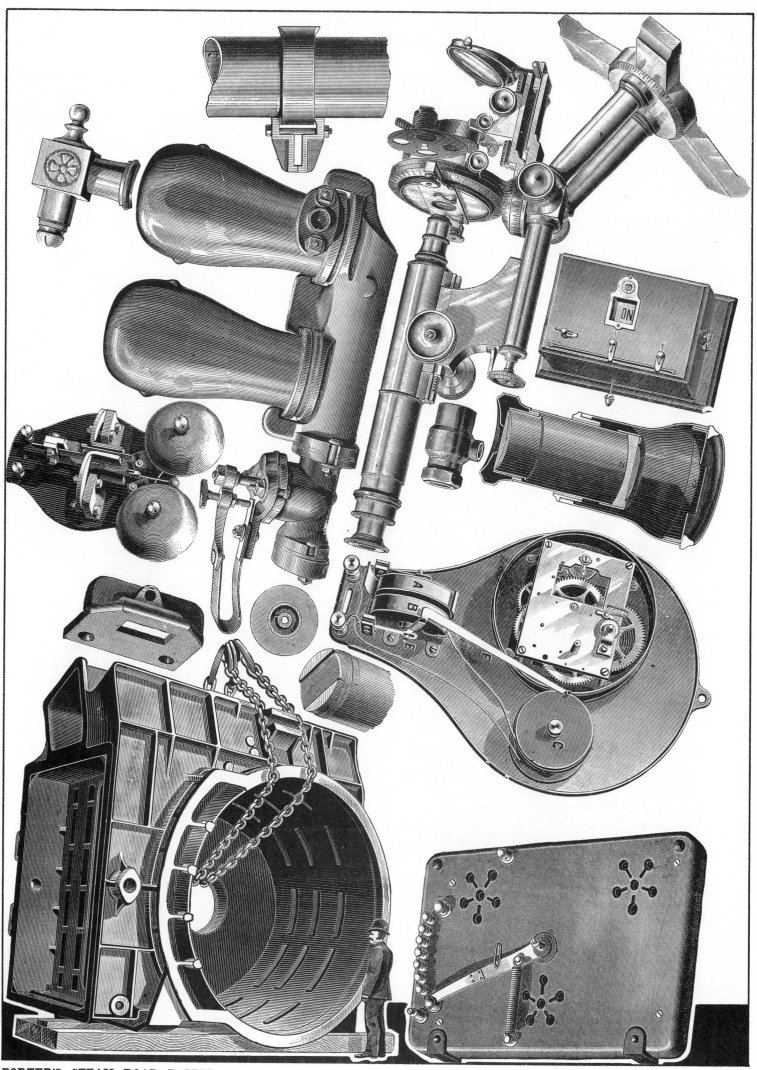

MILLER'S PATENT SCREW HOISTING MACHINE.

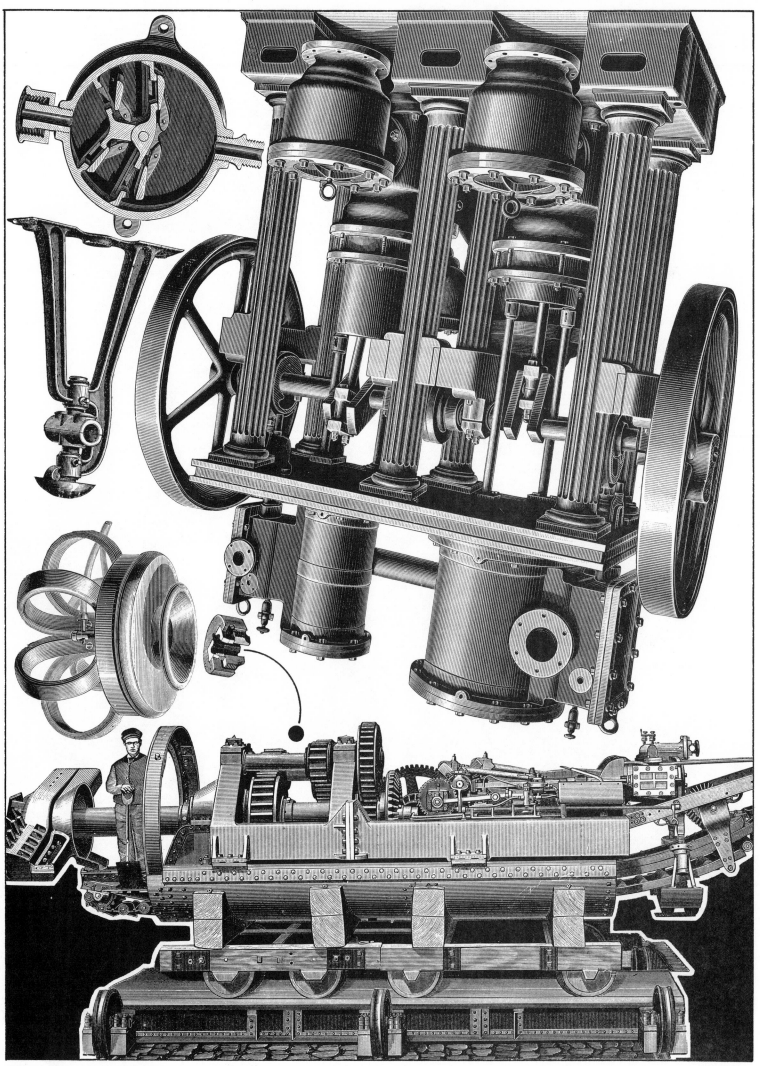

BULLOCK'S SELF-FEEDING AND PERFECTING PRESS.

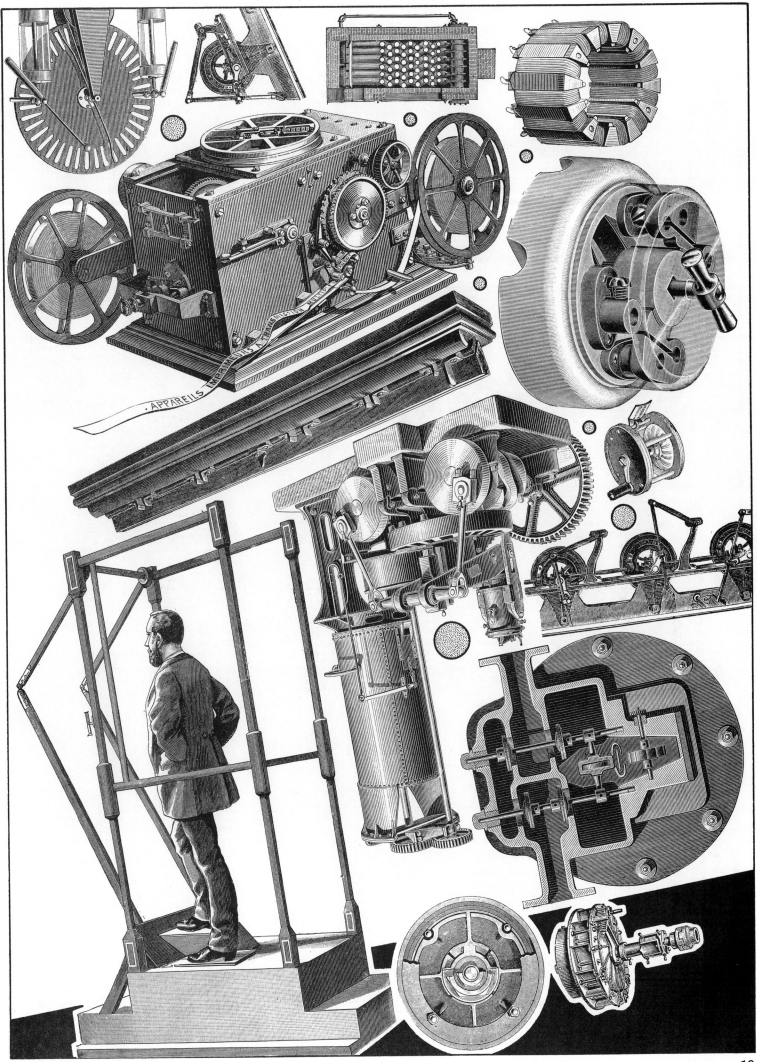

APPAREILS IMPRIMEURS À TRANSMISSION

COOK'S IMPROVED DEVICE FOR LAYING OUT SASHES.

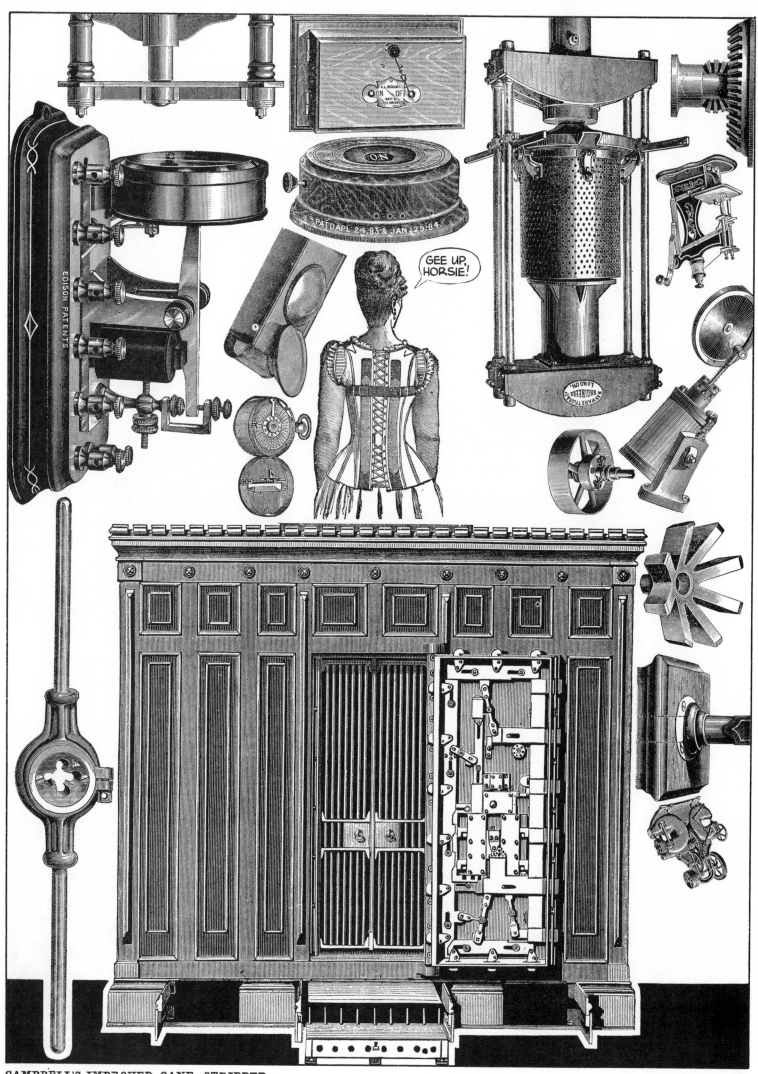

CAMPBELL'S IMPROVED CANE STRIPPER.

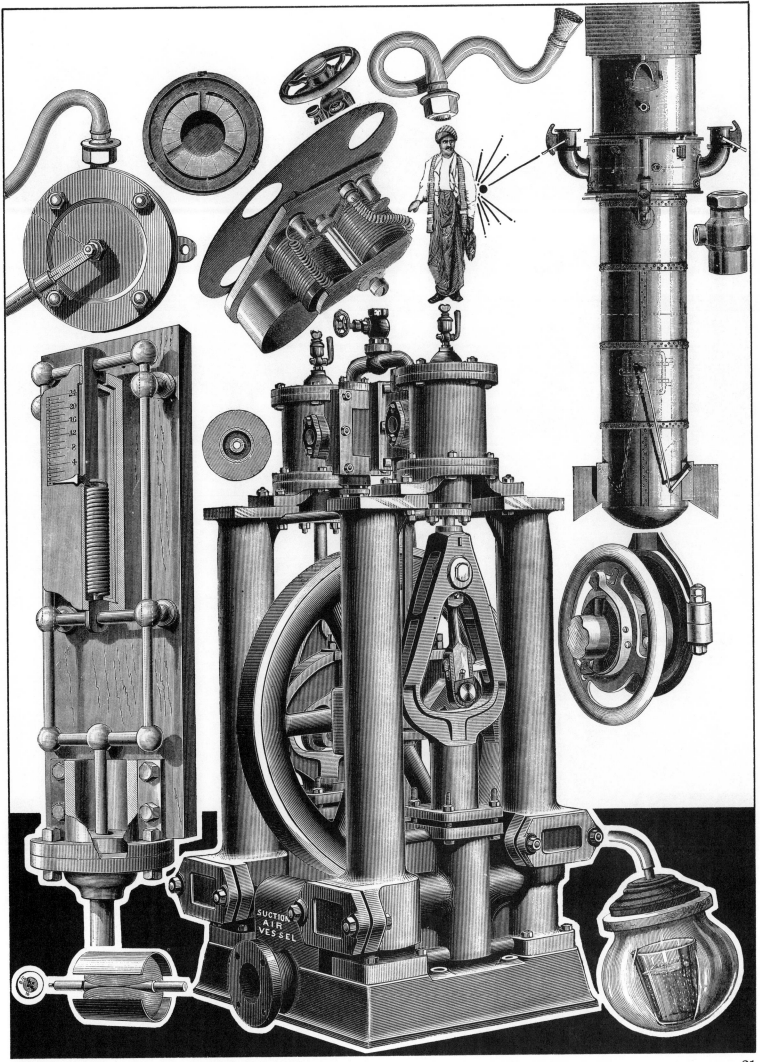

WORTHINGTON'S DUPLEX PRESSURE PUMP.

CHEVALIER AND BRASS' WIRE CRADLE.

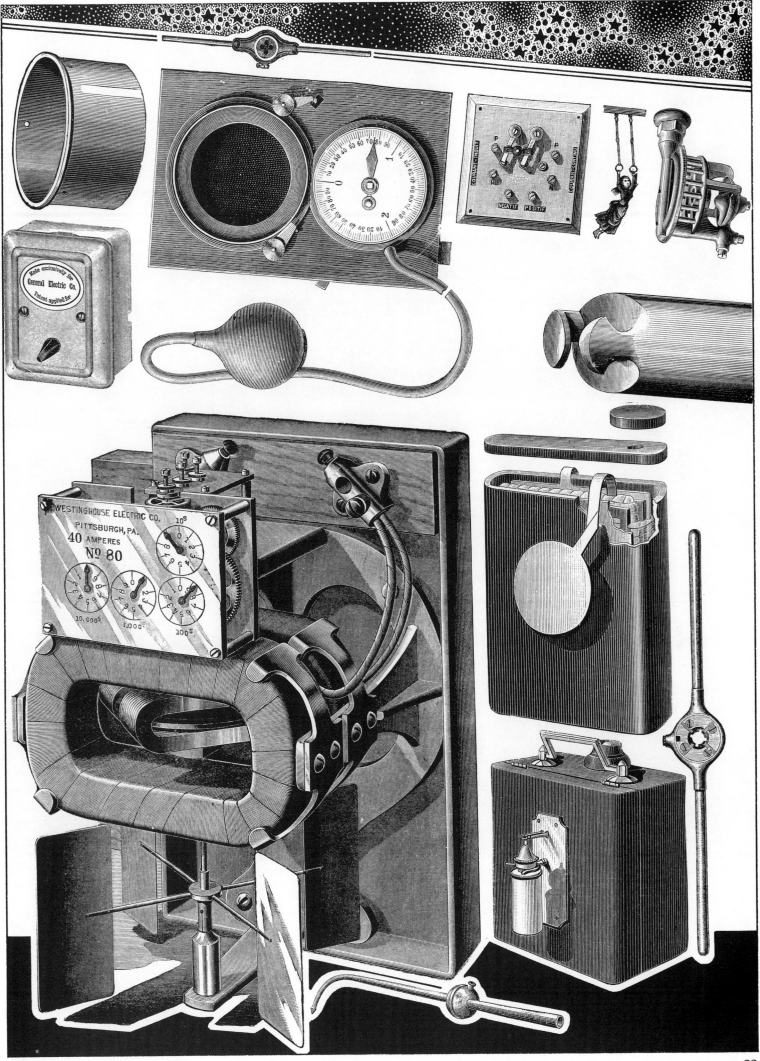

IMPROVED RAPID CUPOLA.

SPAYTH'S RAFTER SCALE AND BEVEL GAGE.

THE IMPROVED GATLING GUN.

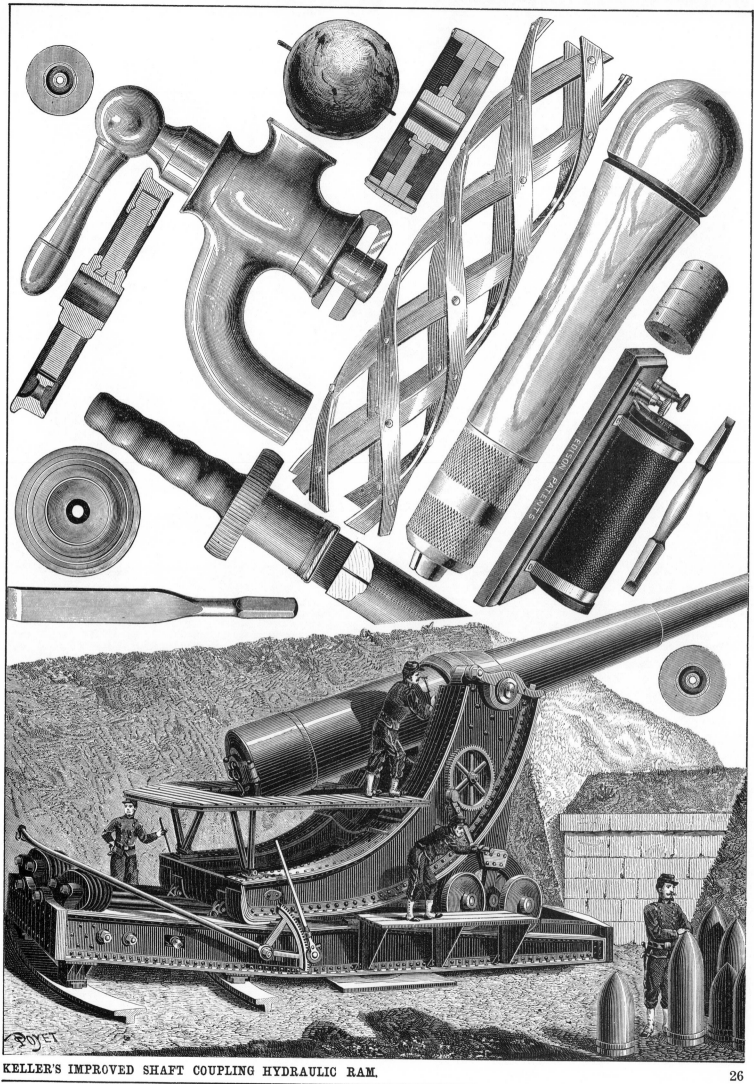

KELLER'S IMPROVED SHAFT COUPLING HYDRAULIC RAM.

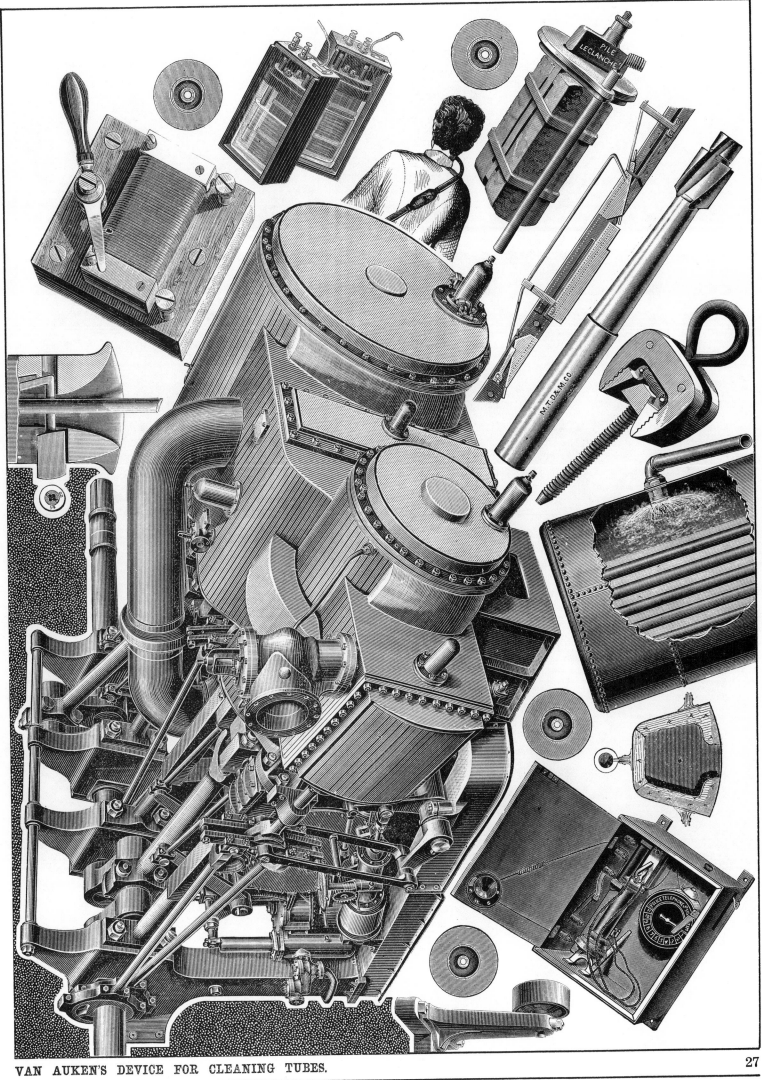

VAN AUKEN'S DEVICE FOR CLEANING TUBES.

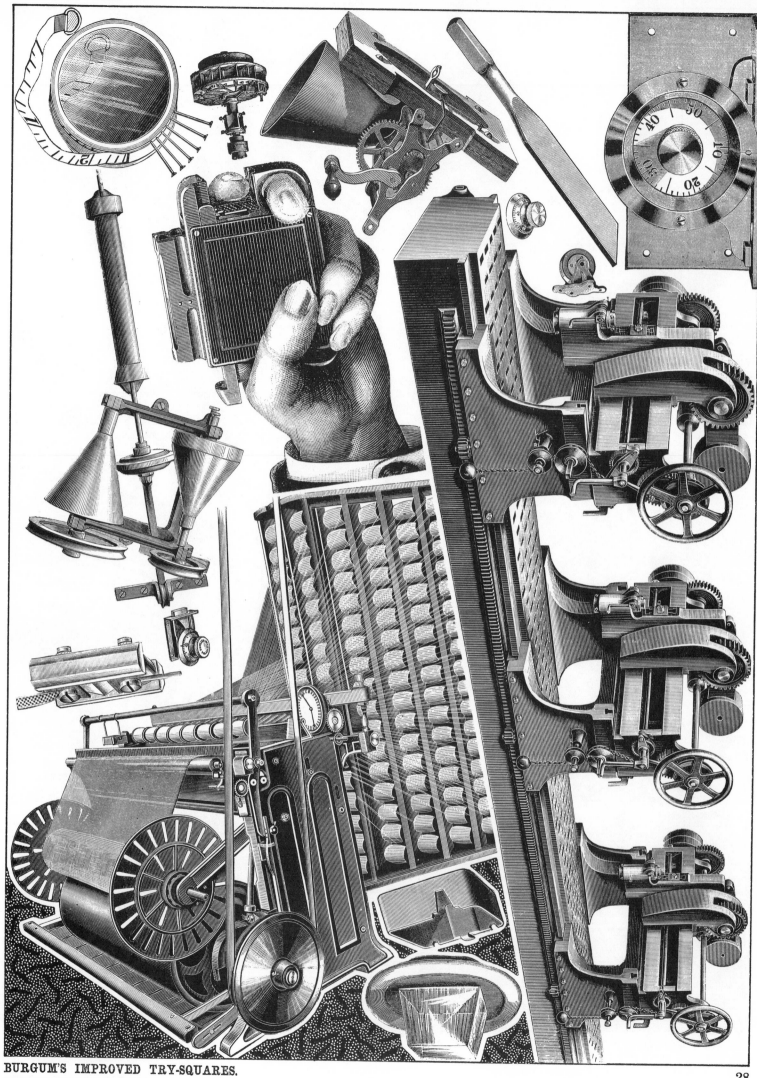

BURGUM'S IMPROVED TRY-SQUARES.

BULLOCK'S STEREOTYPE SHAVING MACHINE.

CRAIK'S IMPROVED TURBINE PRESS FOR TREATING BEET PULP.

BENNETT'S APPARATUS FOR UTILIZING HEAT.

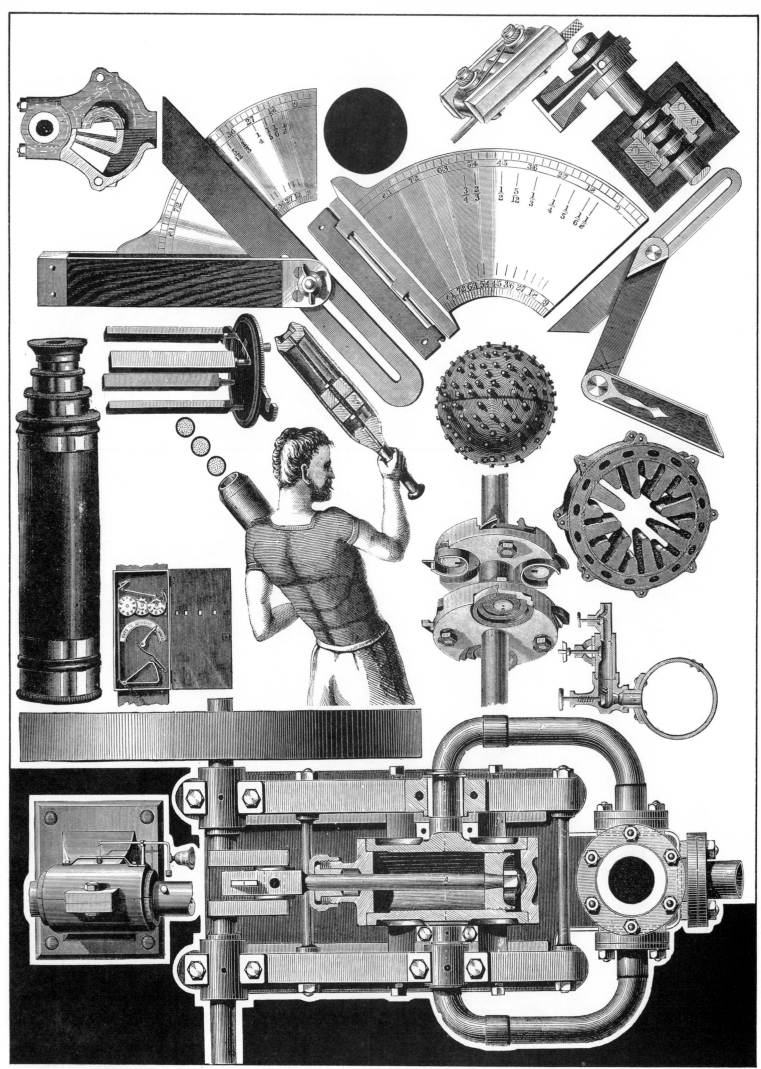

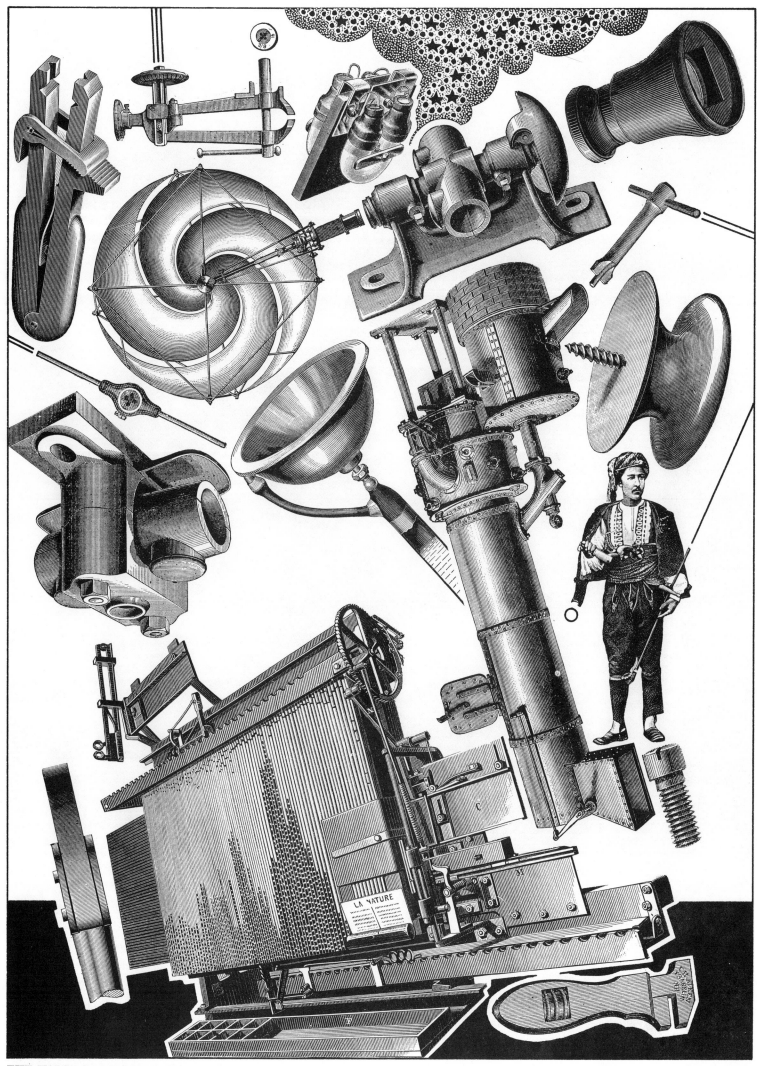

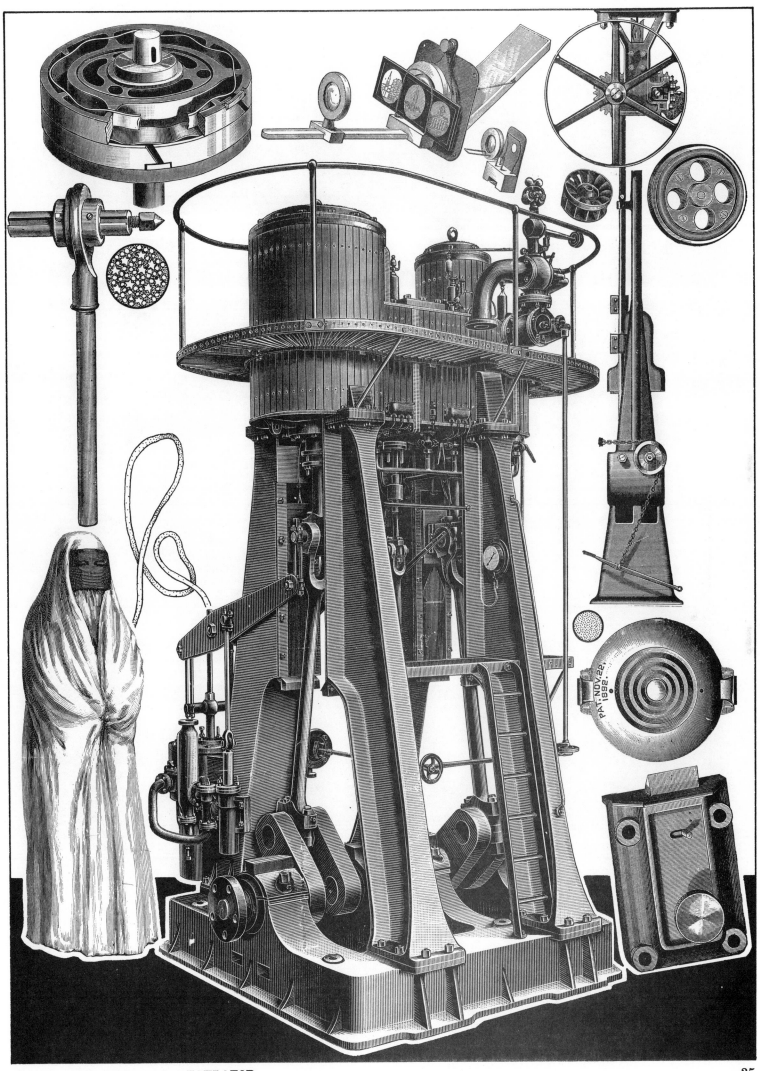

ADAMS' IMPROVED GAS REGULATOR.

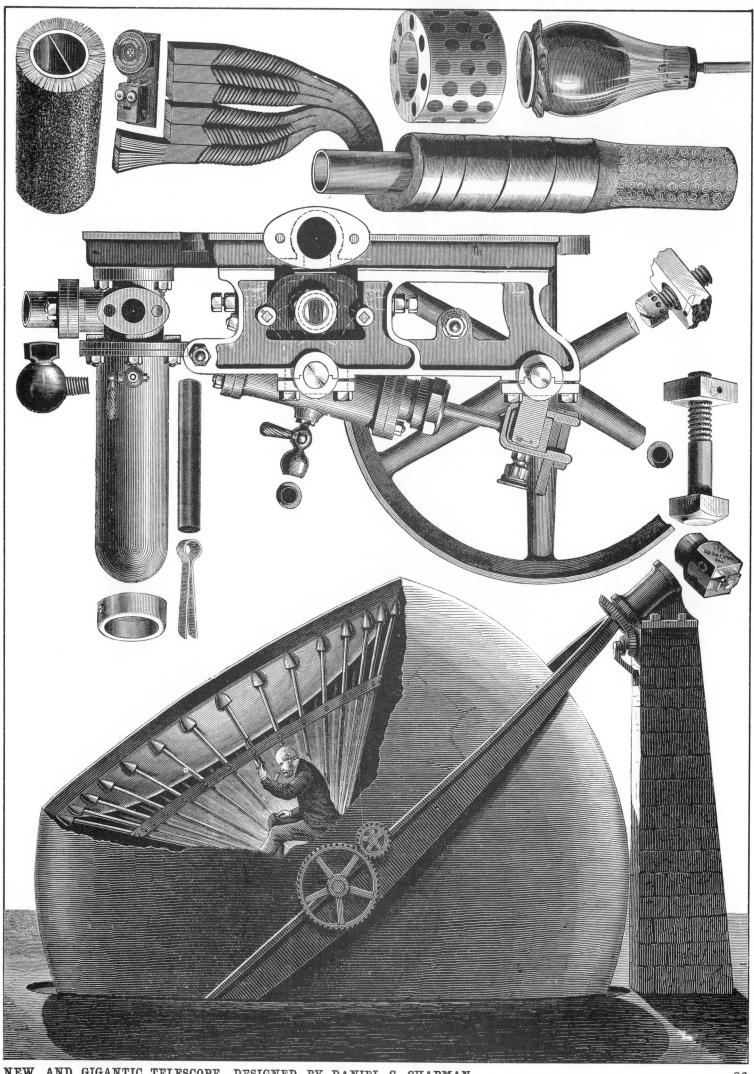

NEW AND GIGANTIC TELESCOPE. DESIGNED BY DANIEL C. CHAPMAN.

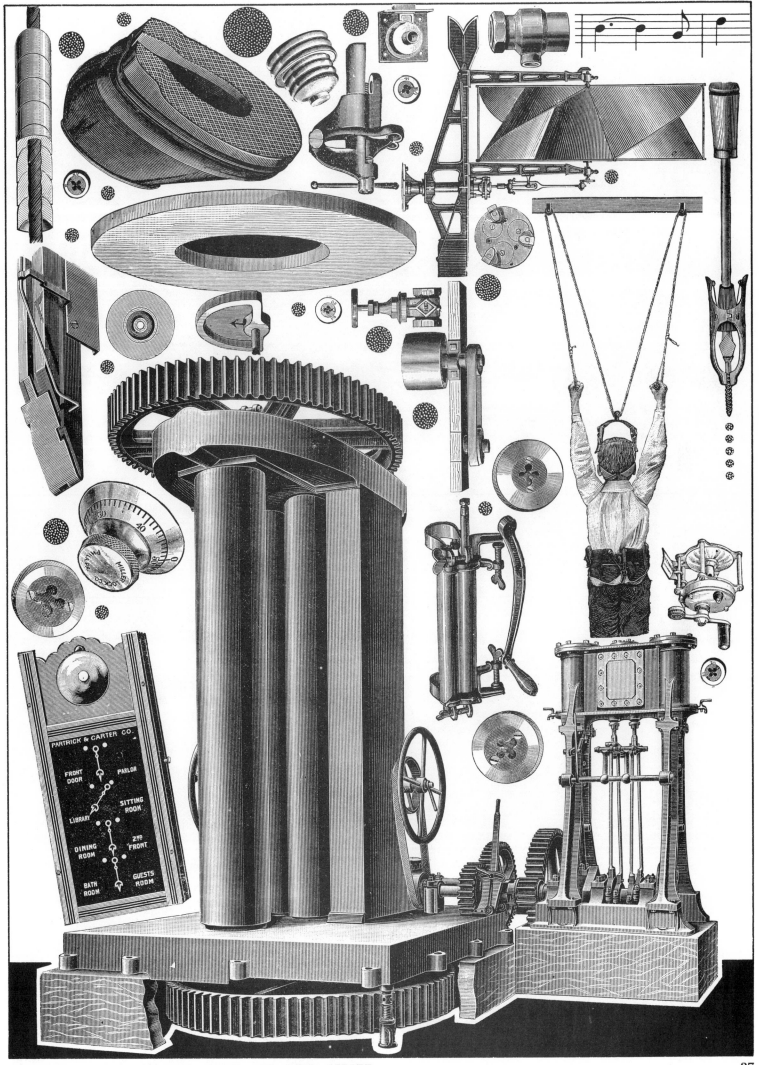

REMINGTON DROP HAMMER WITH DETACHED LIFTER.

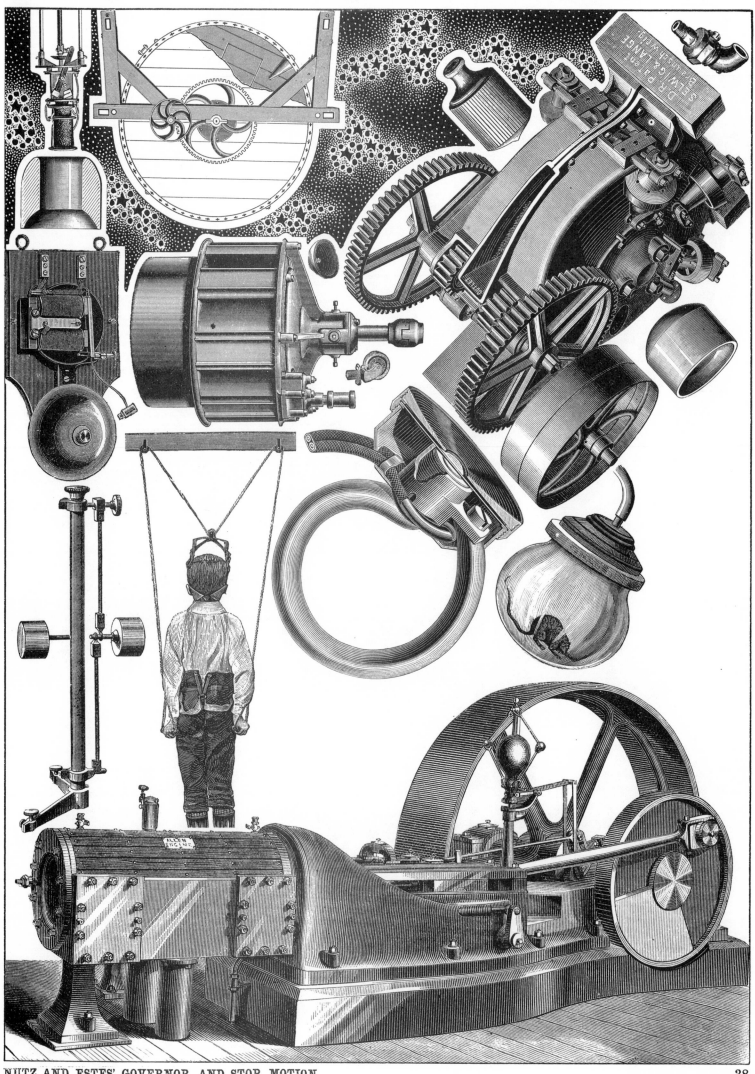

NUTZ AND ESTES' GOVERNOR AND STOP MOTION.

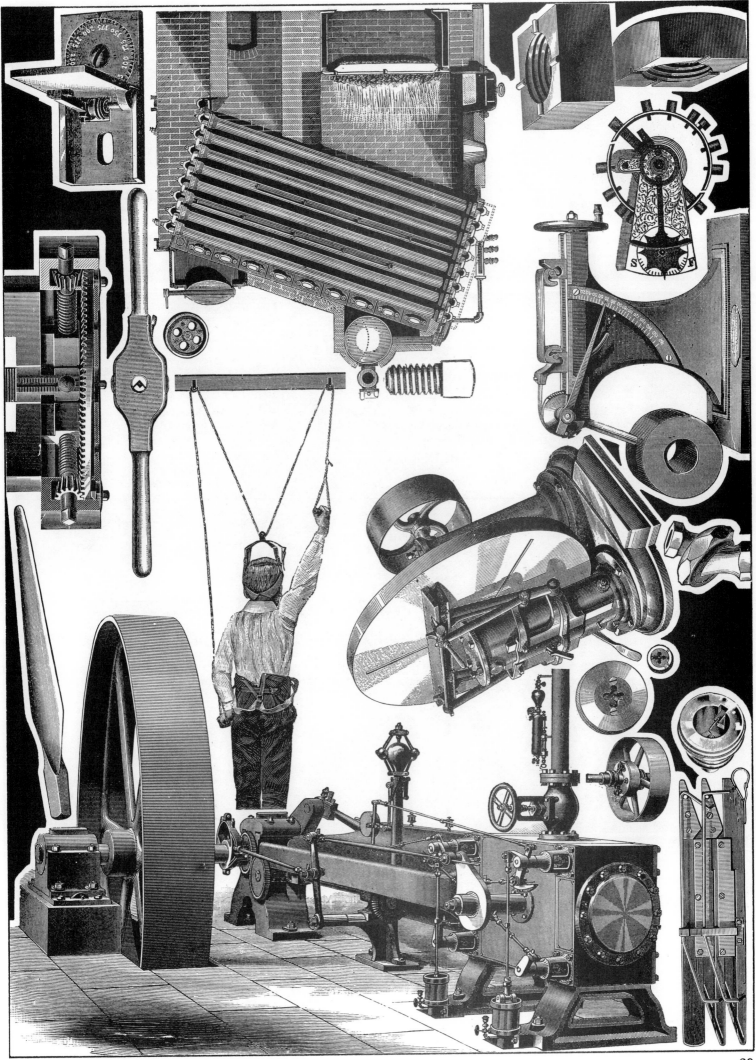

SMITH'S FLOUR-BOLT KNOCKER.

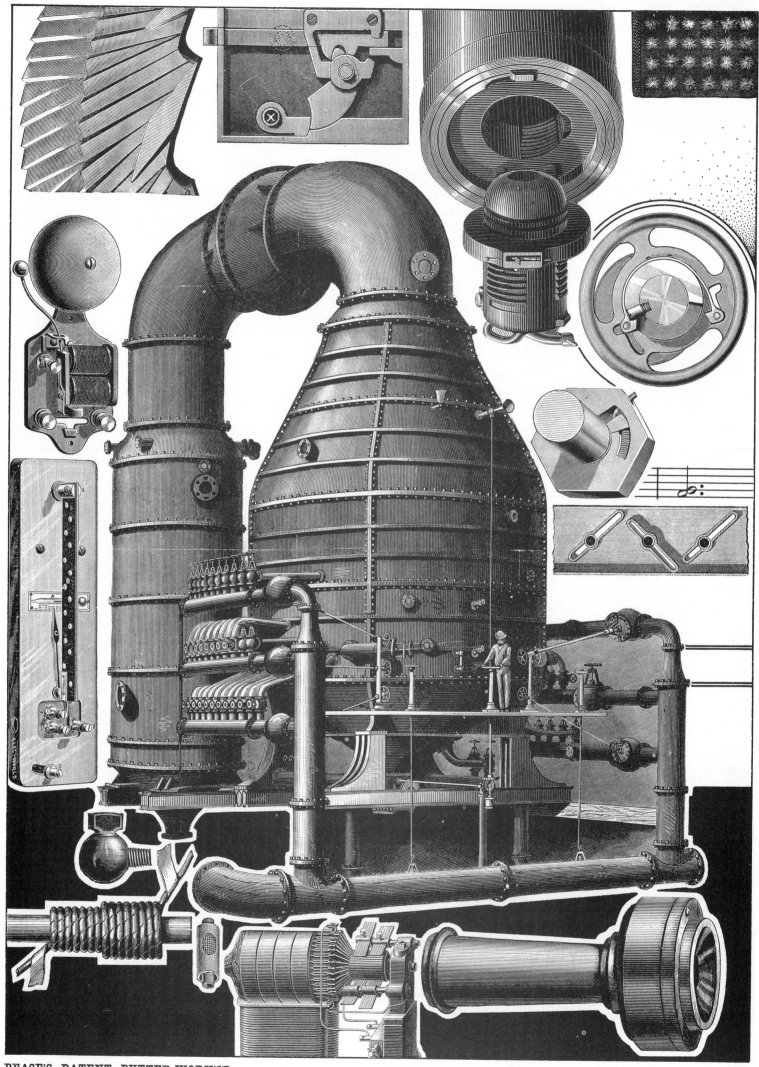

PEASE'S PATENT BUTTER-WORKER.

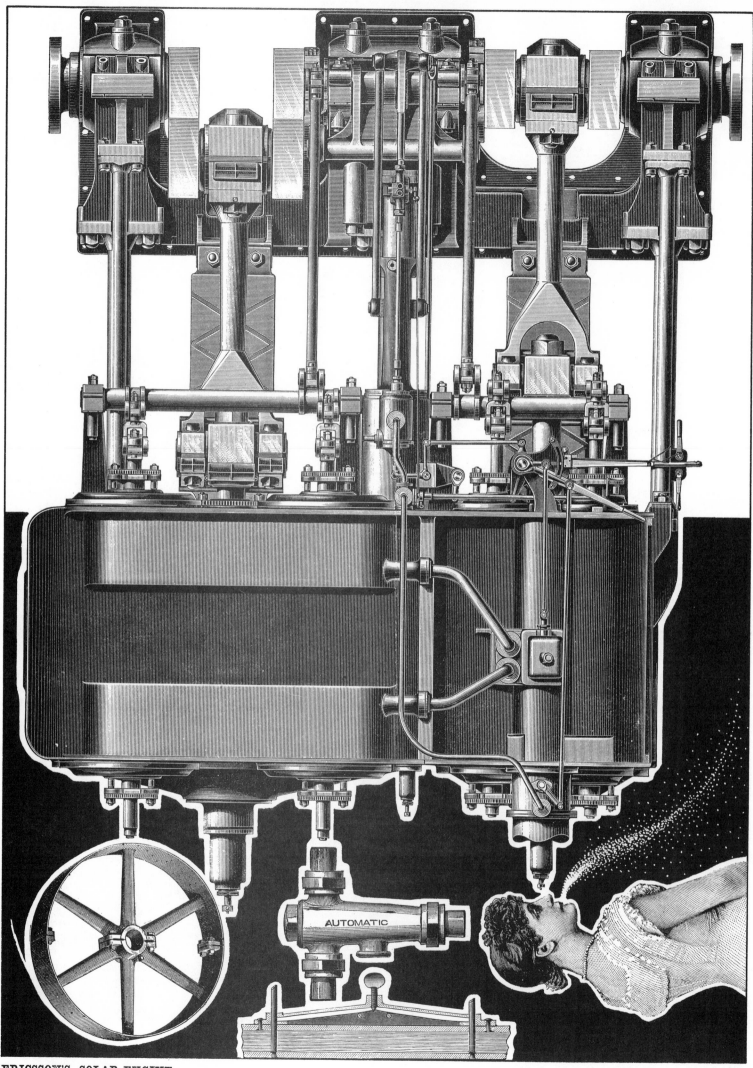

ERICSSON'S SOLAR ENGINE.

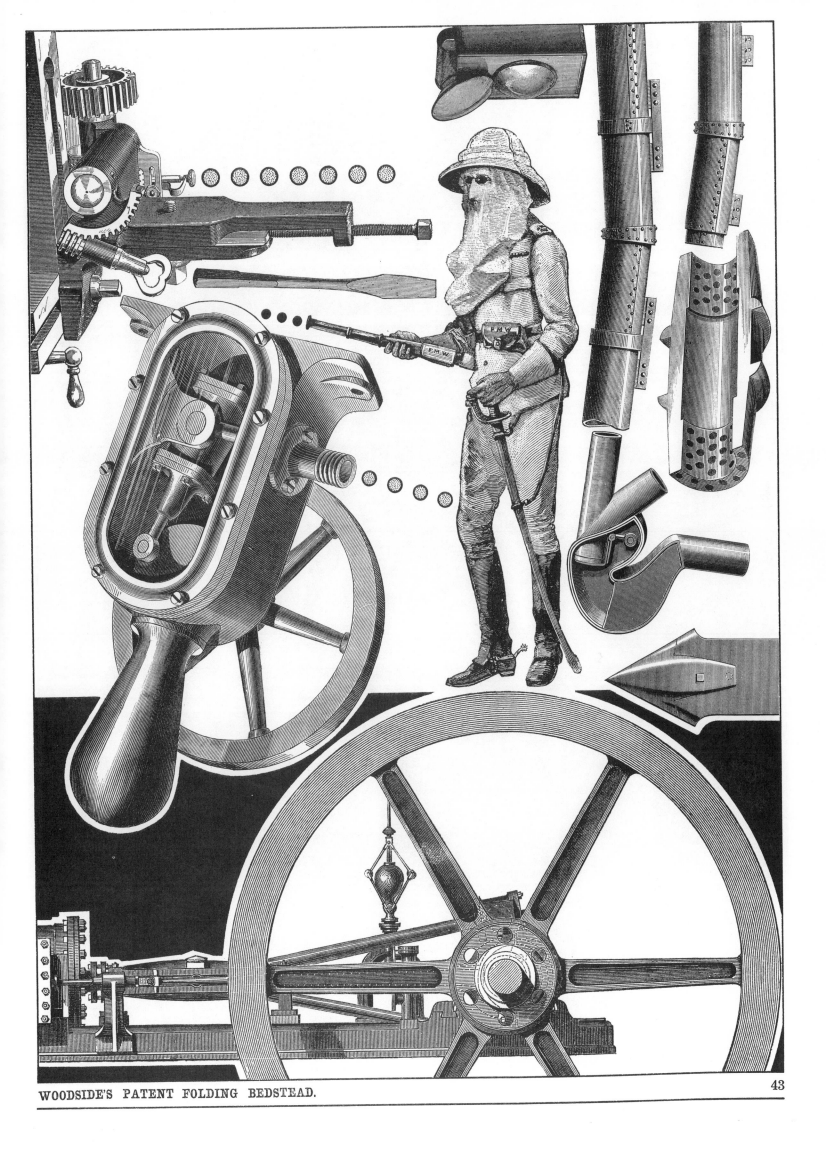

WOODSIDE'S PATENT FOLDING BEDSTEAD.

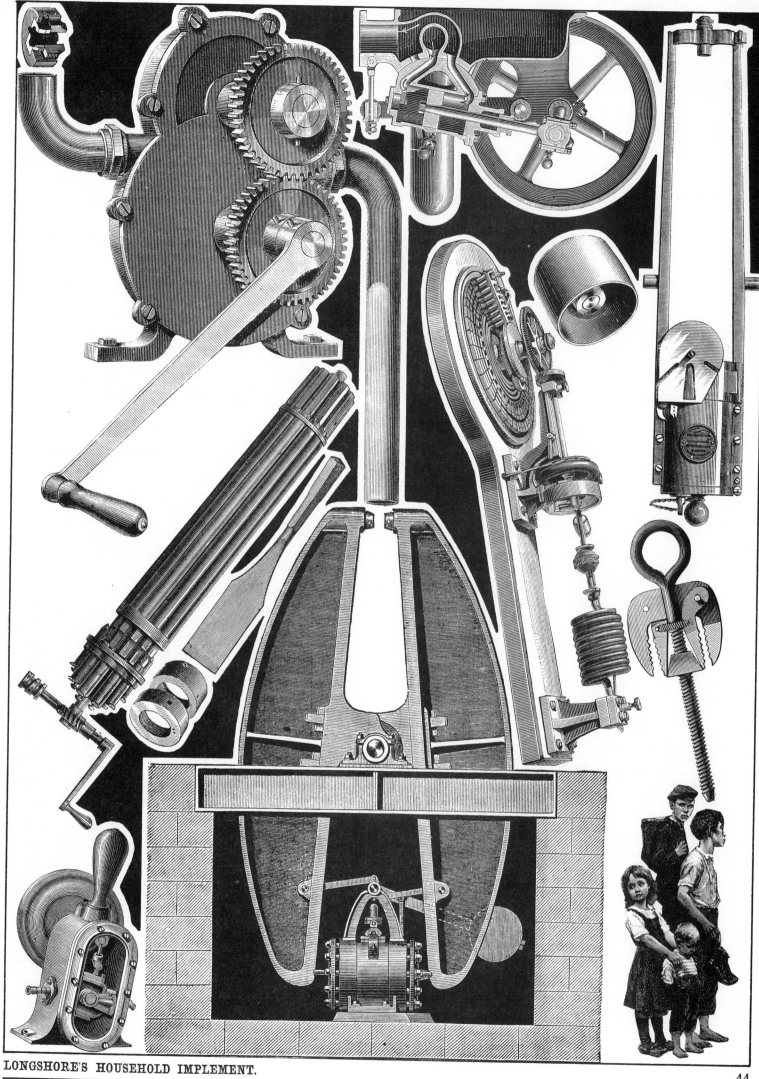

LONGSHORE'S HOUSEHOLD IMPLEMENT.

FONTAINE'S AERO-STEAMER AND SELF-MOVER.

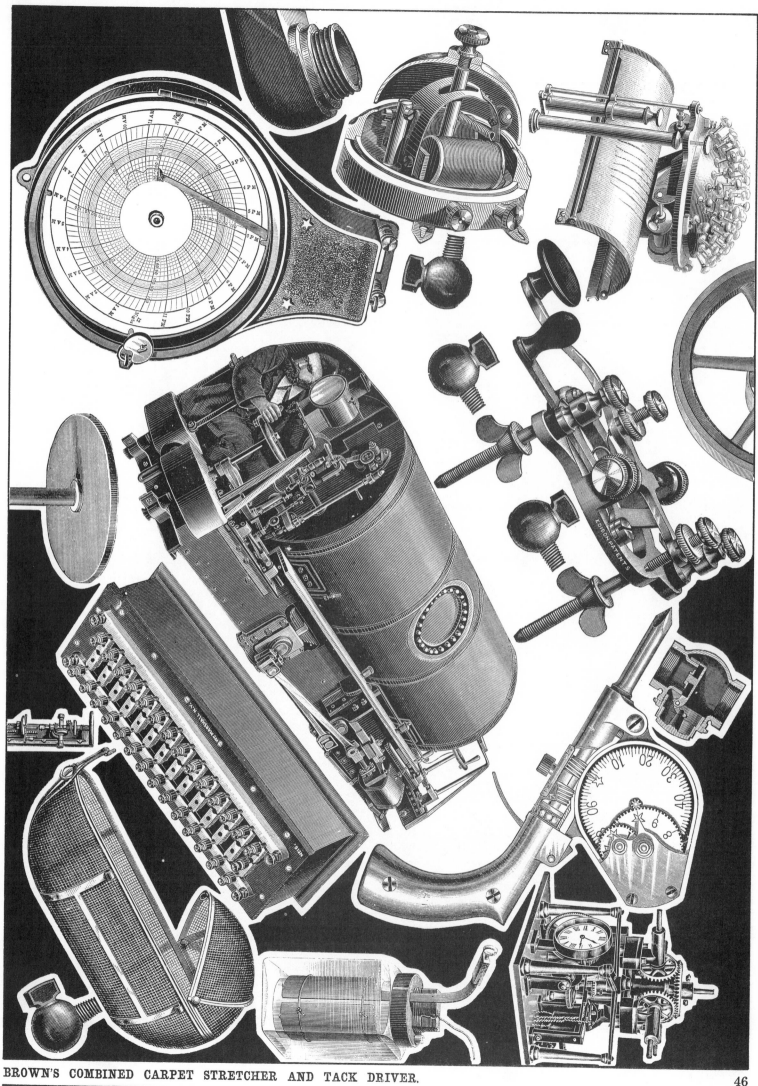

BROWN'S COMBINED CARPET STRETCHER AND TACK DRIVER.

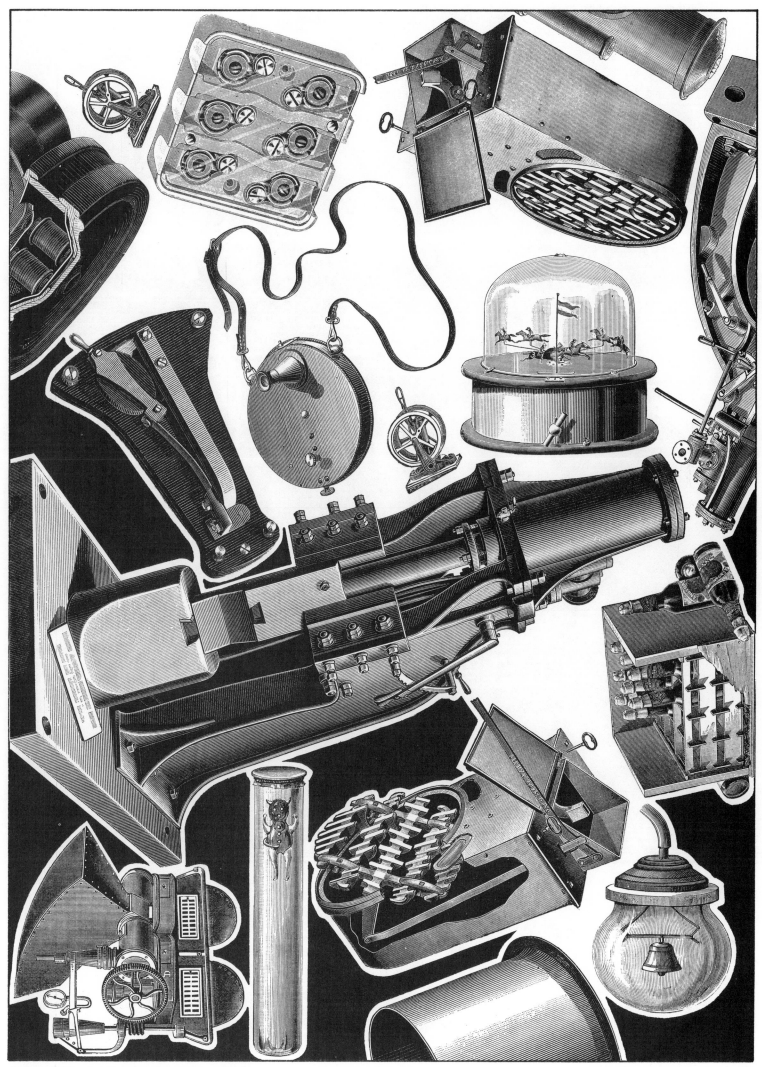

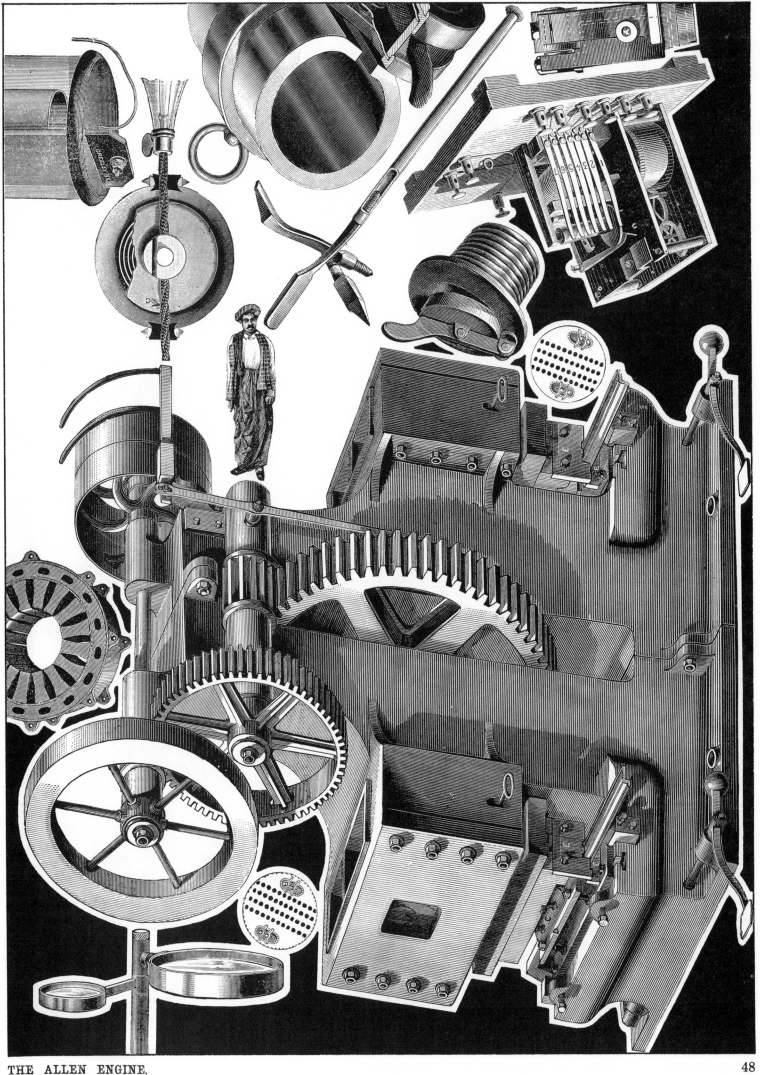

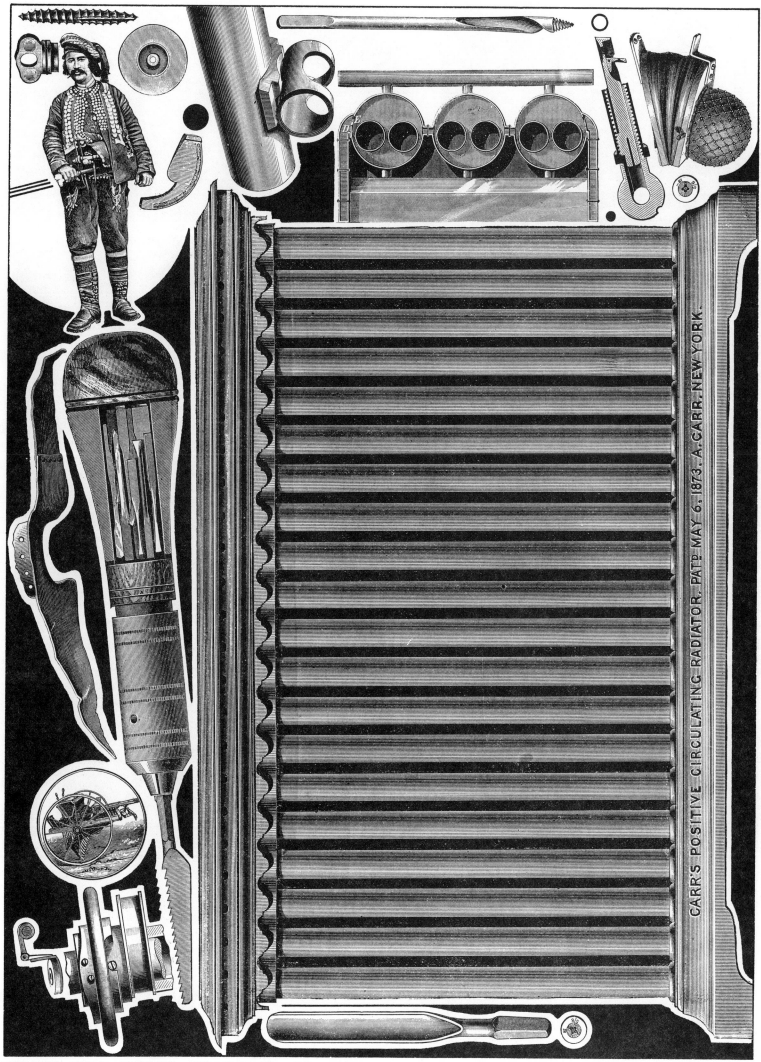

GARR'S POSITIVE CIRCULATING RADIATOR. PAT'D MAY 6, 1873. A. GARR. NEW YORK.

HOPKINS' GEAR CUTTING ATTACHMENT FOR LATHES.

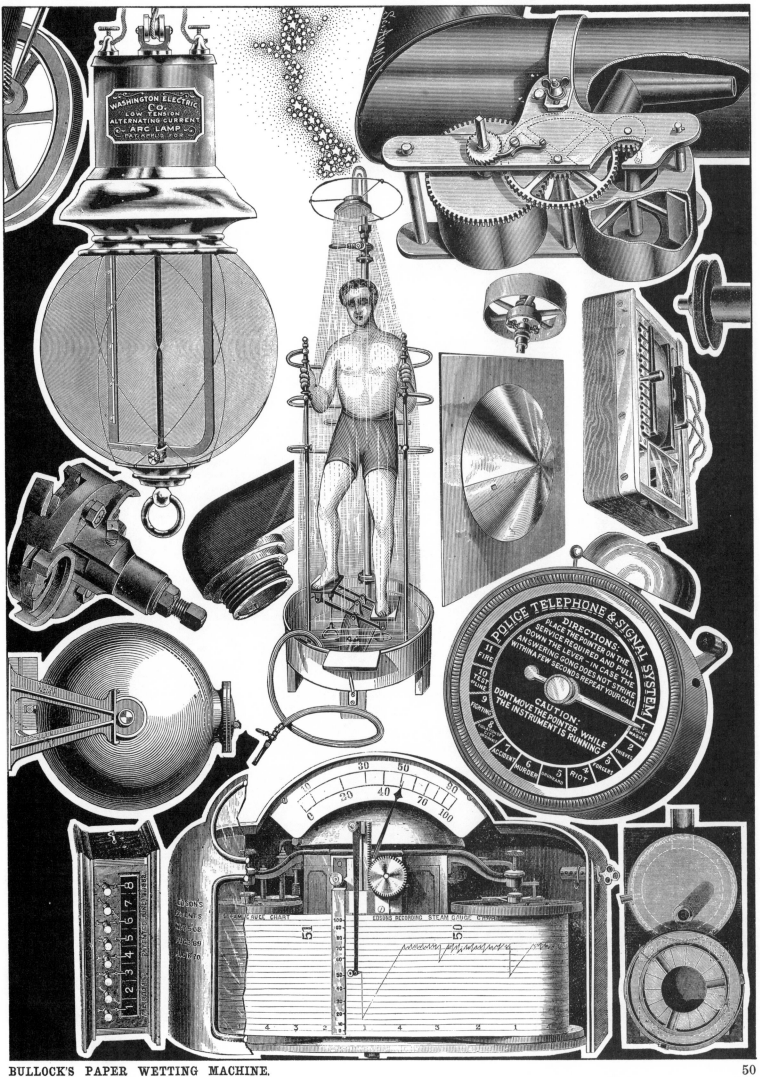

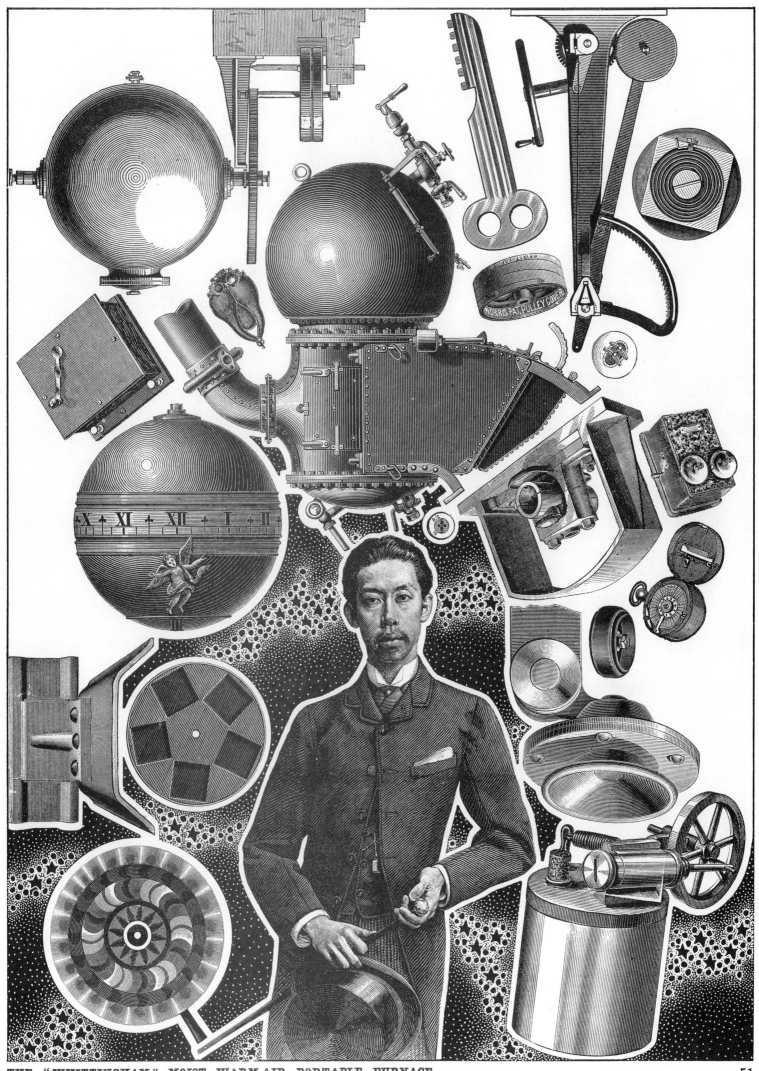

THE "WHITTINGHAM" MOIST WARM-AIR PORTABLE FURNACE.

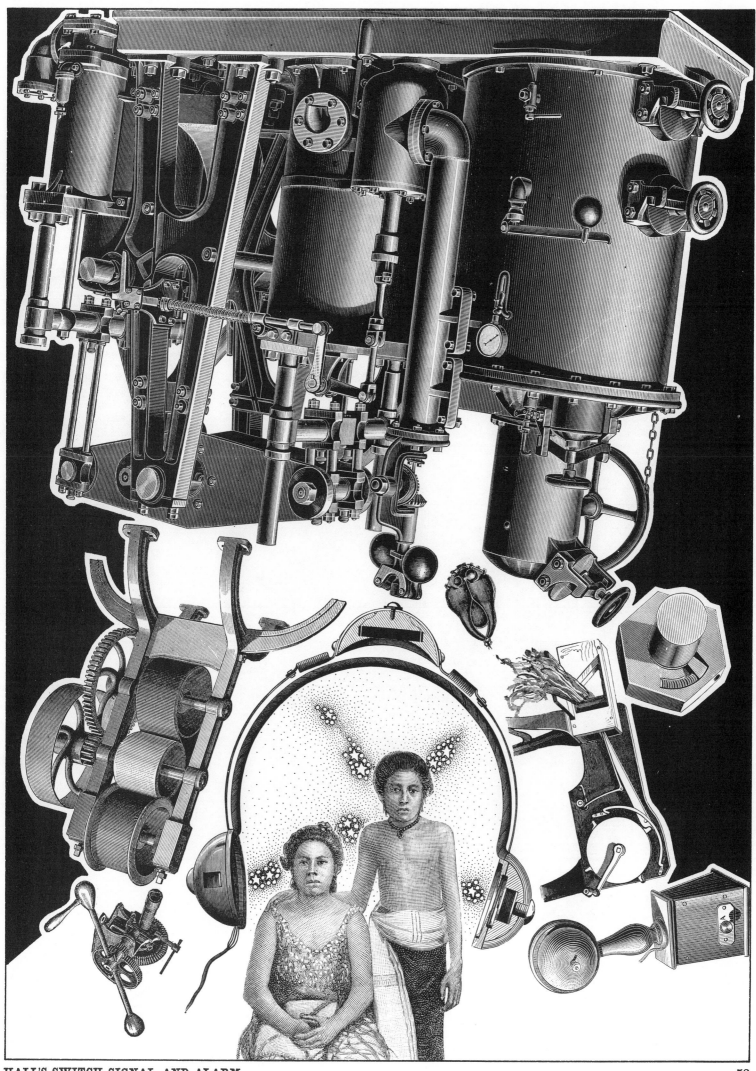

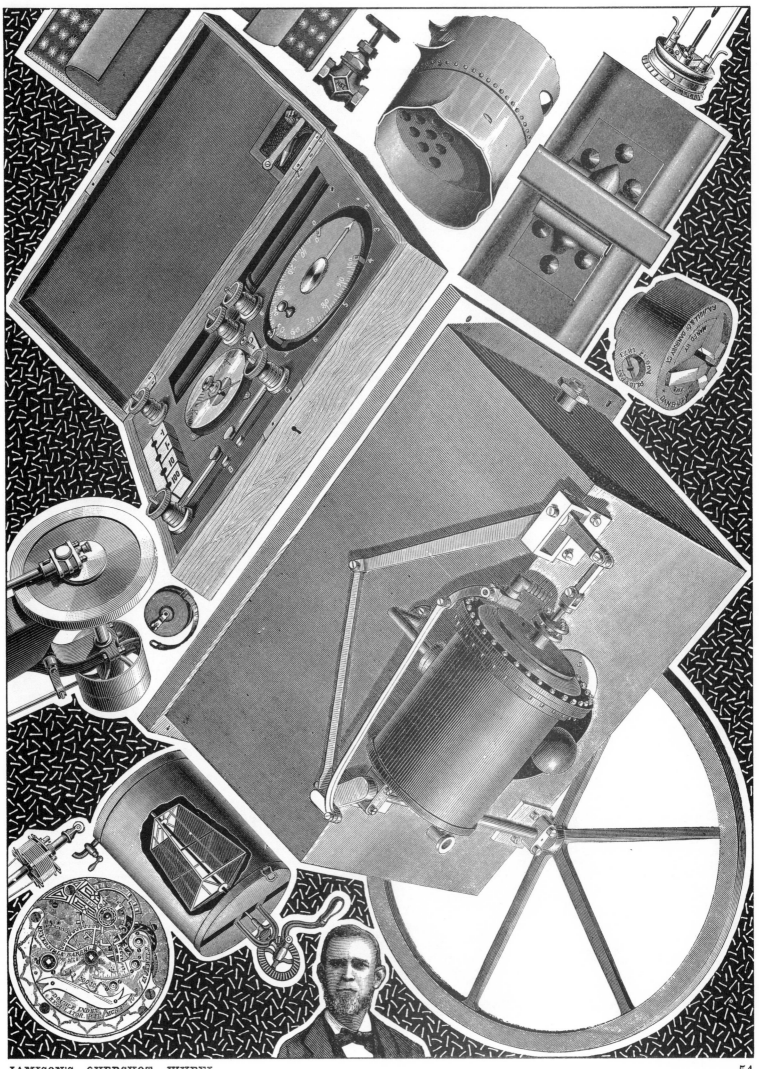

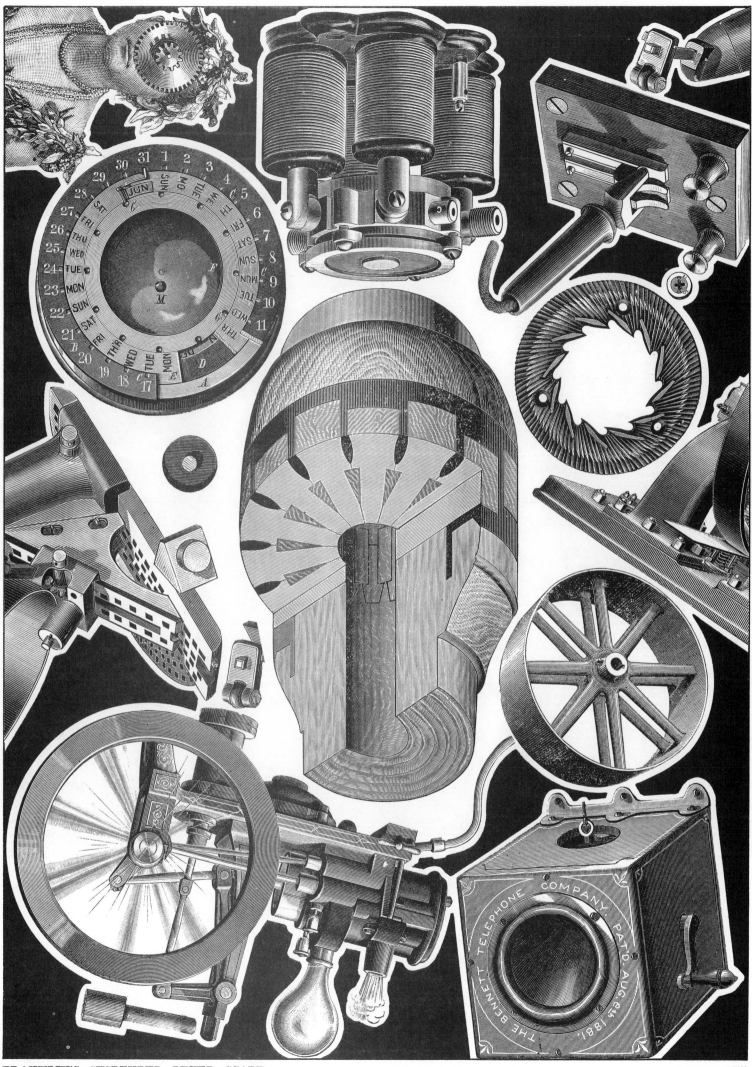

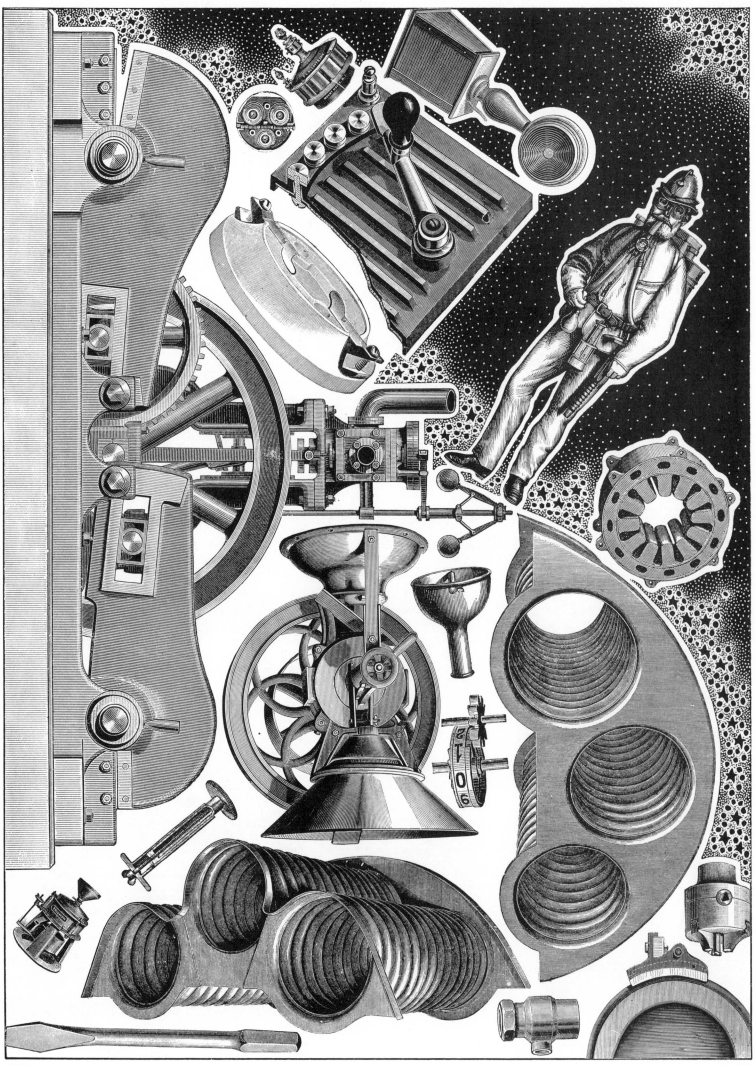

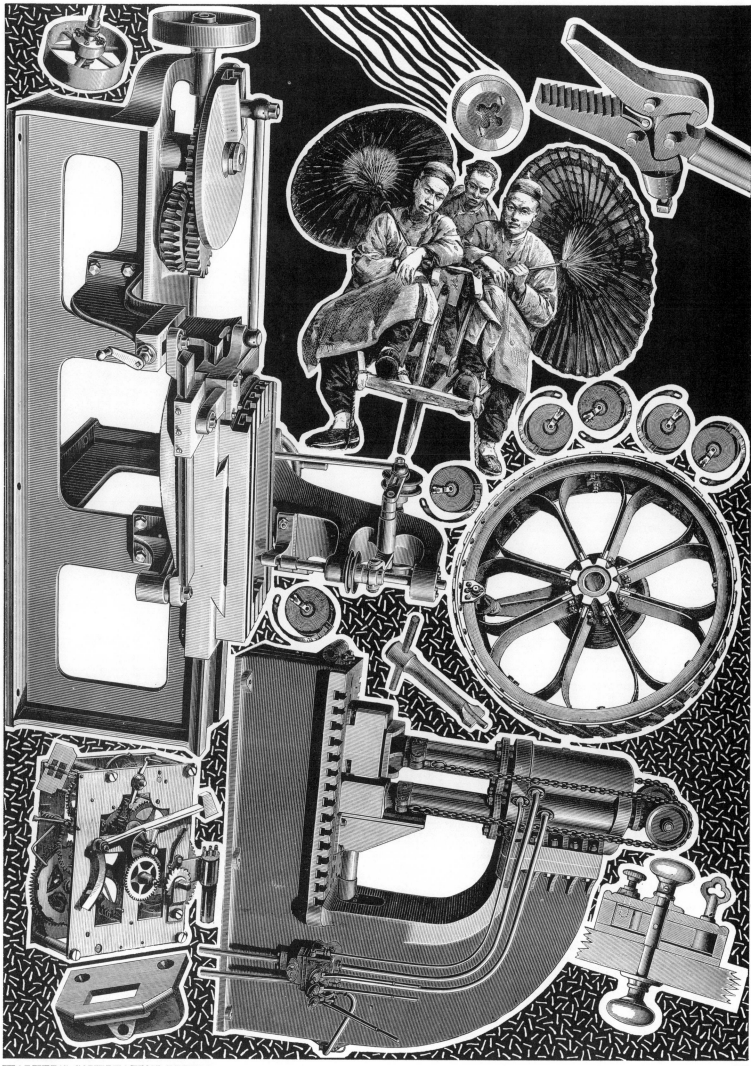

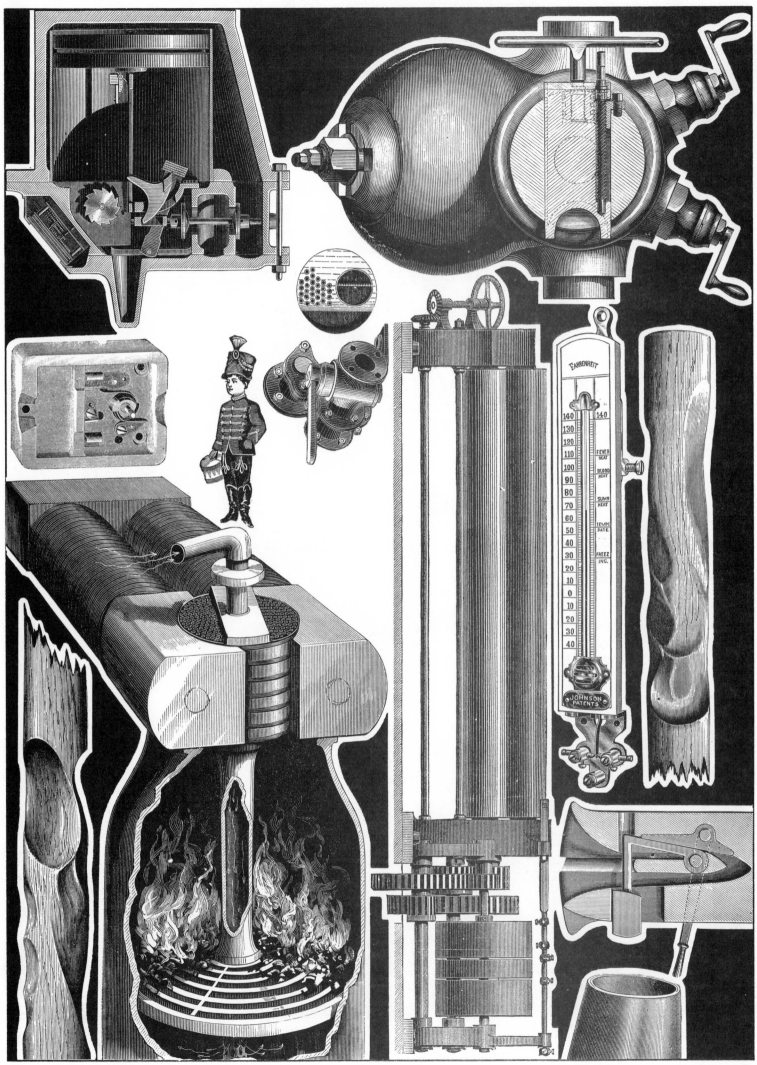

STARRETT'S MEAT AND VEGETABLE CHOPPER.

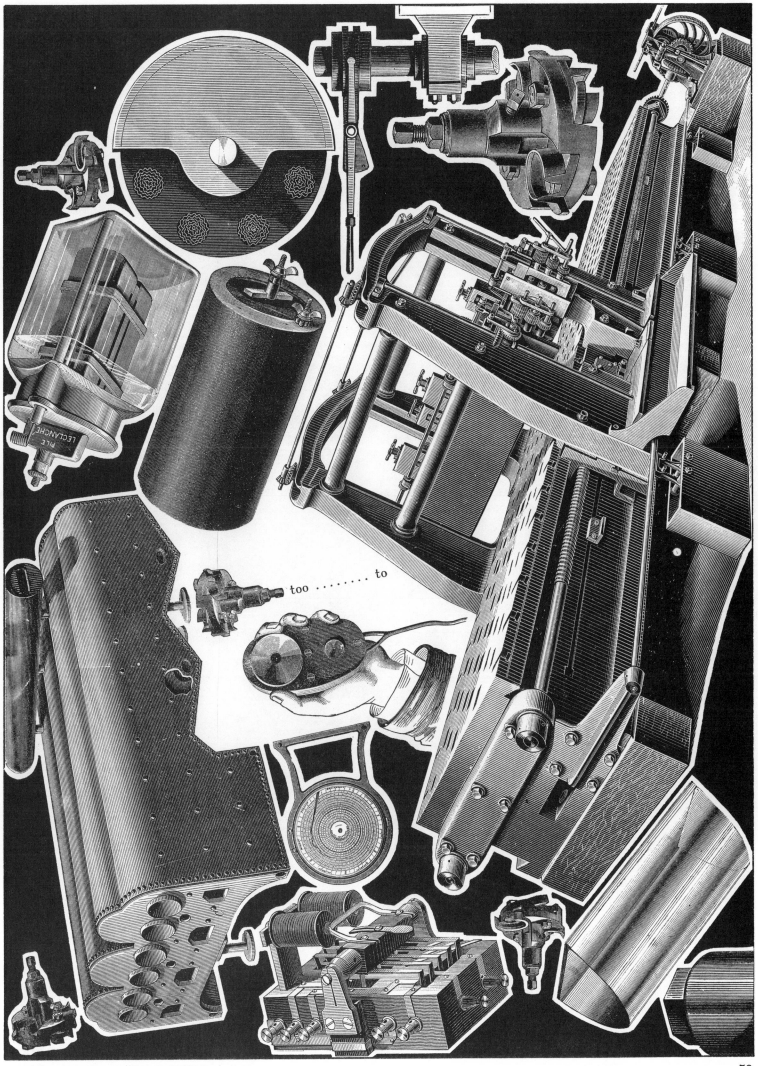

too .... to

AN IMMENSE VACUUM PAN FOR SUGAR MAKING.